Tax Reform in Disequilibrium Economies

Tax Reform in Disequilibrium Economies

SERGE WIBAUT

The right of the
University of Cambridge
to print and sell
all manner of books
was granted by
Henry VIII in 1534.
The University has printed
and published continuously
since 1584.

CAMBRIDGE UNIVERSITY PRESS

Cambridge
New York New Rochelle Melbourne Sydney

Published by the Press Syndicate of the University of Cambridge
The Pitt Building, Trumpington Street, Cambridge CB2 1RP
32 East 57th Street, New York, NY 10022, USA
10 Stamford Road, Oakleigh, Melbourne 3166, Australia

First published 1989

Printed in Great Britain by The University Press, Cambridge

British Library cataloguing in publication data

Wibaut, Siege
Tax reform in disequilibrium economies
1. Taxation
I. Title
336.2

Library of Congress cataloguing in publication data

Wibaut, Serge.
Tax reform in disequilibrium economies.
Originally presented as the author's thesis
(Ph.D.) – Université catholique de Louvain, 1986.
Bibliography.
Includes index.
1. Taxation – Belgium – Econometric models.
1. Equilibrium (Economics) – Econometric models.
I. Title.
HJ2786.W53 1988 336.2′05 88-11861

ISBN 0 521 35588 5

MC

To my parents

Contents

Figures

Tables

Preface and acknowledgements

This book is based on a Ph.D. thesis I presented at CORE (Université Catholique de Louvain) in March 1986. The work involved is part of a vaster programme, financed by the Belgium Government, aiming to show that quantitative economics is not only a game which members of the academic community like to toy with, but that it can also be a useful tool in the hands of the everyday practitioner. So, and at the risk of adding one more paving-stone of good intentions to the road leading to hell, this book is about deriving rules to help the public decision taker to levy taxes more efficiently.

Tax reform, and its elder brother optimal taxation, are however complex and technical matters. These features are unfortunately unavoidable and even though the decision rules provided here are relatively simple and appealing, their derivation requires more than often a fair amount of formalisation. This, I think, should not discourage the potential reader: proofs are usually meant to be skipped!

Someone once said that acknowledging a debt is like drawing up the guest list for a wedding: you either invite only the best man or you invite everyone. I am afraid I have very many best men: the enthusiasm and kindness of all CORE members helped to make this research enjoyable and fulfilling. I am however first of all indebted to Henry Tulkens, my thesis supervisor, who struggled patiently through earlier versions of this text. I wish to thank Jacques Drèze, Roger Guesnerie, Maurice Marchand, Louis Phlips and especially Per-Olov Johansson whose comments and suggestions helped me to clarify many problems and improve the presentation of this monograph. I also benefited from several conversations with my ex-colleagues at Université Laval. So many thanks to Fabienne Henry and Elizabeth Pecquereau to whom I imposed the cruel experience of deciphering my crawly handwriting. Their patience in doing so was only equalled by their skilful typing. Finally, I would like to give special thanks to my wife Dominique whose constant presence and understanding has proven to be one of the most gratifying aspects of this work.

1 Introduction

1.1 Optimal taxation and tax reform

One may define an optimal tax system in several ways. According to Sandmo (1976) there are three obvious criteria for optimality which in fact depend greatly on the observer's nature. The first, which is often a primary concern of the tax administrator, demands that the tax system minimises the cost involved in collecting and paying the taxes. The second requires the tax system to be fair. This aspect is probably the main preoccupation of every ordinary tax payer. Unfortunately no one up till now, from Plato to Rawls, has been able to come up with a definition of justice on which unanimous agreement could be reached! Finally, one can think of the optimal tax system as being the most efficient one, i.e. 'the one which minimises the aggregate deadweight loss for any given tax revenue or level of public expenditure' (Sandmo, 1976, p. 37).

Efficiency is by nature the domain of economists and in the field of welfare economics it often amounts to adopting the concept of Paretian efficiency, i.e. a state of the economy such that moving away from it would make at least one agent worse off. The Pareto criterion is obviously controversial since 'a society or an economy can be Pareto optimal and still be perfectly disgusting' (Sen, 1970, p. 22); yet it has survived criticisms and most of its critics.

With respect to this criterion, it is well known that lump-sum taxes are neutral because they do not affect the agents' marginal evaluations. It is however difficult to imagine lump sums as being a permanent source of revenue to the government without them becoming an income tax scheme in a disguised form. Once it is admitted that this form of taxation cannot reasonably be implemented, one faces the second-best problem of finding the 'best' tax vector in a price-distorted economy.

The first formalised treatment of the second-best optimum appeared in the now classical article by Ramsey (1927). However elegant it might be, this analysis aroused little interest from other economists.[1] One had to wait for Boiteux' contribution (1956) for a revival of interest in the subject in Europe (see Drèze, 1964). It took more than another decade for these ideas to cross the Atlantic and for them to give birth to articles such as those by Baumol and Bradford (1970) and Diamond and Mirrlees (1971). These successive contributions gave the subject its 'lettres de noblesse' and consequently recognition within the academic community.

More recently, and for reasons which will become clearer later on in this work, much attention has been focused on the problem of defining, given an existing tax system, welfare improving tax movements. Such movements have been labelled in the literature 'directions of tax reform' (see Guesnerie, 1977). Instead of looking for the tax formulae that characterise a second-best optimum, one tries in the reform problem to identify 'small' tax moves which are feasible and satisfy some given criterion. Guesnerie proved that unless the economy is already at a second-best optimum, such moves may always be found. He also noted that they may sometimes result in a temporary abandonment of production efficiency.

1.2 Disequilibrium theory

Quite independently of this evolution in taxation theory, economic thought has lately focused on the theory of so-called disequilibrium states of market economies. As is now clear, the keystone to Keynes' theory of income and unemployment consists of the assumption that, in the short run, prices and wages may not be flexible enough to clear all markets in the economy. In other words, and contrary to Walrasian and Marshallian beliefs, price movements may not be sufficient to guarantee that the economy always moves from one general equilibrium to another, in both of which all resources are fully employed. The assumption of price rigidity emanates from the factual observation that, although fast adjustments of prices may still prevail on some specific markets (those for raw materials for instance), nothing similar happens on the markets for services or manufactured goods. Moreover the downward rigidity of wages has long been recognised and need not be commented on any further. It appears therefore that the first, and often main, signals of discrepancies between supply and demand are to be found in quantity adjustments such as waiting lines, bottlenecks and, more dramatically, unemployment.

These considerations have given rise to many models of partial equilibrium which try to explain unemployment. Only lately, however, has it been widely recognised that general equilibrium is the proper

[1] One can only note a simplified treatment of Ramsey's work in Pigou's book on public finance (1947) and in a paper by Samuelson (1951).

approach to the problem and that one cannot expect to explain what is happening on one market without knowing what is going on on the others (see, for instance, Barro and Grossman, 1971 or Malinvaud, 1977). In this spirit Malinvaud proposes to distinguish between three main types of disequilibrium situations – or 'regimes' – for market economies. They are illustrated in Figure 1.1.

In all of these regimes it is assumed that prices are rigid and that quantities are determined by the short side of each market at those prices. Differences between regimes are based upon whether excess demand or excess supply prevails on the goods- and on the labour markets. The Keynesian unemployment regime is thus characterised by excess supply on both markets for goods and for labour. On the other hand, when labour is not fully employed and firms are not rationed on the market for goods, the regime is called 'classical unemployment'. Finally, when demand exceeds supply on both markets, there is latent inflation repressed by the price rigidities and the regime is that of 'repressed inflation'.

1.3 Outlook of this work

This study has both a theoretical and an empirical objective. First, we wish to unify some existing works concerning second best and tax reform theories and to incorporate these in a disequilibrium context. Secondly, at the empirical level, we hope to identify and numerically estimate desirable directions of tax reform for a particular country at a given point of time, namely Belgium in 1982, and evaluate whether there are 'many' or only a 'few' such directions.

		Market for goods	
		$D<S$	$S<D$
Market for labour	$D<S$	Keynesian unemployment	Classical unemployment
	$S<D$		Repressed inflation

Figure 1.1 Disequilibrium regimes

The model we consider in this book tries to be simple but realistic enough. Households may consume goods produced by the private sector and a commodity produced by a state owned monopoly. They supply labour and hold shares in the profits of the private sector. This sector imports one input and exports part of its production. The government taxes labour and the consumption of the private commodities. It also fixes the price of its own production. Lump-sum transfer policy is not considered for the sake of realism. The government's aim is to find a vector of consumer prices (or equivalently, a level of consumption) which maximises social welfare.

Considering public production surely adds a zest of cost-benefit analysis to the model. Although the derivation of project evaluation rules is not the primary goal of this study, it will soon appear that the shadow prices (i.e., the way households' utility is affected by a marginal change in their consumption) to be used by governments when evaluating a project are a by-product of our results.

Rather surprisingly, a great deal of the cost-benefit analysis literature implicitly assumes quantity rationing and fixed prices (although very few authors dare to admit they commit such a heresy!). This is particularly true as to the way labour is treated in standard text books dealing with project evaluation (see, for instance, Dasgupta *et al.*, 1972). On the other hand, this literature mainly analyses partial equilibrium situations, revealing thereby its inability to find a link between Keynesian macroeconomics and microeconomic analysis. Fix-price theory provides such a link. Indeed, and as we shall see later, one can derive second-best and shadow-pricing rules, which are functions of the standard Keynesian multiplier, starting from the usual utility and profit maximisation problems. This result is important and goes far beyond the sole second-best interpretation: it means that macroeconomic multiplier effects emerge quite naturally from a framework based on individual choice behaviour. As stated by Drèze (1984, p. 46): '. . . the quest for microeconomic foundations of macroeconomics is replaced by the discovery of macroeconomic implications of microeconomics'.

This book is organised as follows: in Chapter 2, we start by assuming that prices are fully flexible (i.e., markets clear by price movements) and by deriving a characterisation of the second-best solution as well as the existence conditions of directions of tax reform for such an economy. We go on to examine the relevance of the fixed-price approach in explaining the way actual economies behave. We then derive, for several cases of quantity rationing, second-best and tax reform solutions and try to present the results in terms of easily interpretable and estimable formulas.

Chapter 3 is devoted to the study of several algorithms for determining whether directions of tax reform exist under given characteristics of the economy and, if so, for computing some of them. These algorithms, which rely on standard linear programming techniques, may also be used to build the whole set of these directions.

In the first section of Chapter 4, we determine which employment regime was prevailing in Belgium in the early eighties. The available information seems to suggest that most firms were mainly constrained by demand and therefore the observed unemployment was due to aggregate demand slackness, which implies a Keynesian regime. We then briefly examine the general economic situation in Belgium in order to get some idea of the extent to which price and wage changes could have an impact on the main macroeconomic aggregates. In the following sections, we estimate all the relations necessary for the computation of directions of tax reform: a demand system for consumption goods with a rationing on the labour market, an export function, a transition matrix establishing the link between the consumption and the production sectors, and labour demand functions for the private and the public production sectors.

These estimations are used in Chapter 5 in which we enquire if the existence conditions of directions of tax reform obtained in Belgium in 1982. The model considers the taxation of labour services and of seven consumer goods. The consumption sector is characterised in terms of assumed preference characteristics of ten typical consumers. Empirical evidence suggests that, at that time and for this level of aggregation, directions of tax reform increasing the ten agents' utilities and leaving the public sector's accounts unaffected could be found. After having constructed the set of these directions, we exhibit next those directions that are the 'best' ones with respect to alternative social welfare functions which vary according to some 'inequality aversion' parameter. It appears that these advocated directions are relatively sensitive to the distributional options made but that their implementation may have a fairly small impact on the macroeconomic aggregates such as consumption and labour demand.

The last chapter contains concluding remarks bearing upon our results and various suggestions for further work.

2 Tax reform and disequilibrium models

2.1 The economy

We consider an economy with $N+1$ consumer goods, the first N of which (indexed by $i=1,\ldots,N$) are supplied by the private sector whereas the last one is produced by the public sector. There is also a $N+2$nd good which is imported but is used in the production process only. This economy is composed of H households, indexed by $h=1,\ldots,H$. Each household consumes quantity x_i^h $(i=1,\ldots,N)$ of the privately produced goods and z^h of the publicly produced good; it also supplies homogeneous labour in quantity l^h. We denote by C^h the actual consumption bundle of agent h, i.e. $C^h=(x^h, z^h, -l^h)\in \mathbb{R}^{N+2}$.

The following notation will prove useful

$$x=\sum_h x^h, \qquad z=\sum_h z^h, \qquad L=\sum_h l^h.$$

Consumers face a price vector $q=(q_x, q_z, q_l)$, where q_x is itself a N-dimensional vector. The price of the ith private good, q_{x_i}, includes a tax so that $q_{x_i}=(1+t_{x_i})p_{x_i}$ where t_{x_i} is the tax rate and p_{x_i} the production price. The second component of C^h, q_z, is simply the price at which the public sector sells its production. The third component, q_l, is the net wage rate, i.e. $q_l=(1-t_l)p_l$, t_l being the tax rate on labour income and p_l the gross wage rate.

Each agent receives a share θ^h $(\sum_h \theta^h=1)$ of the private sector's profits, π. For notational convenience we denote $r^h=\theta^h\pi$. The budget constraint faced by agent h may thus be written as

$$q'C^h=r^h \tag{2.1}$$

Finally agent h's preferences are represented by the twice continuously differentiable utility function $u^h(C^h)$ which is monotonic and strongly quasi-concave in its arguments.

The private sector is treated as an aggregate, i.e we only consider the production vector for society (see Arrow and Hahn, 1971, p. 62) and not the individual firms' production functions. This assumption allows us to avoid specifying how, in the disequilibrium model, individual firms are affected by the rationing scheme. The private sector uses two inputs, i.e. labour l^p and a good m which has to be imported (raw material for instance), in order to produce its output. The amounts of the latter are denoted by the N components y_i of the production vector y. Let $s=(y, -l^p, -m)$. Part of the output y_i $(i=1, \ldots, N)$ is supposed to be exported. We denote this quantity e_i but assume for simplicity that it is exogenously fixed.

The private sector faces a certain technology represented by the following convex production function

$$F(s)=0. \tag{2.2}$$

Expliciting this function with respect to l^p and y yields the minimal inputs requirement needed to achieve a given level of production, i.e.

$$\begin{aligned} l^p &= l^p(y, m) \\ m &= m(y, l^p) \end{aligned} \tag{2.2'}$$

Finally, the private sector sells its production y_i at prices p_{x_i}, pays labour at p_l and the other input m at p_m. The latter is supposed to be a 'world-price' which is given and fixed; it will serve as numeraire so that we may set $p_m=1$. We denote by p_x the price vector of the privately produced goods (i.e. $p_x=(p_{x_1}, \ldots, p_{x_N})$) and by p the vector of all producer prices ($p=(p_x, p_l, 1)$).

The private sector's profit can be expressed as

$$\pi = p's. \tag{2.3}$$

The last agent of the economy, the public sector, collects taxes on the consumption of the private goods and on labour income. It does not participate in international trade but produces goods Z in quantity z using a technologically determined amount of labour l^z

$$l^z = l^z(z). \tag{2.4}$$

The level of output in the public sector is determined by the agents' demand, i.e. $z=\sum_h z^h$. The net cost of labour for this sector is $q_l l^z$ whilst its production is sold at unitary price q_z. The accounts of the public sector are defined quite naturally as the sum of its receipts minus its expenditure, or

$$S \underset{\text{def}}{\equiv} (q_x - p_x)'x + (p_l - q_l)l^p + q_z z - q_l l^z. \tag{2.5}$$

Defining $L = l^p + l^z$, the right-hand side of (2.5) may be rewritten as

$$q_x'x + q_z z - p_x'x + p_l l^p - q_l L. \tag{2.6}$$

By adding the H consumers' budget constraints and substituting π by its value, one obtains

$$q_x'x + q_z z = q_l L + (p_x'x + p_x'e - p_l l^p - m). \tag{2.7}$$

Combining (2.6) and (2.7) one finds $S = (p_x'e - m)$. This last familiar result simply states that the budget surplus S is equal to the trade surplus, hereafter referred to as B.

2.2 The Walrasian case

This section proceeds as follows: first we characterise the agents' behaviour and the markets' equilibrium in a general, flexible-price framework. Then we study the second-best and tax reform problems for this economy in Sub-Sections 2.2.2 and 2.2.3 respectively. The results obtained in these sub-sections are of interest on their own, but they also prepare for the study of the disequilibrium models as their derivation relies on concepts and techniques which are used in the remaining sections of this chapter.

2.2.1 Individual behaviour and market equilibrium

Each household maximises its utility $u^h(C^h)$ subject to its budget constraint (2.1). This maximisation yields the following demand functions

$$C^h = C^h(q, r^h), \quad h = 1, \ldots, H \tag{2.8}$$

In terms of the indirect utility function $V^h(q, r^h)$ we have by Roy's identity

$$\begin{aligned} \frac{\partial V^h}{\partial q} &= -\varphi^h C^h \\ \frac{\partial V^h}{\partial r^h} &= \varphi^h \end{aligned} \tag{2.9}$$

where φ^h is agent h's marginal utility of income.

The private producer maximises his profits (2.3) subject to the production function constraint (2.2). This optimisation procedure yields the supply functions

$$\begin{aligned} y_i &= s_{y_i}(p), \quad i = 1, \ldots, N \\ m &= s_m(p) \\ l^p &= s_l(p); \end{aligned} \tag{2.10}$$

or in vector notation

$$s = s(p). \tag{2.10'}$$

At the private producer's equilibrium, one has

$$p_{x_i} = p_l \frac{\partial l^p(y, m)}{\partial y_i}, \quad i = 1, \ldots, N$$
$$= \frac{\partial m(y, l^p)}{\partial y_i} \tag{2.11}$$
$$p_l = \frac{\partial m(y, l^p)}{\partial l^p}$$

i.e. producer prices must be equal to marginal costs expressed in terms of the numeraire.

Equilibrium on the markets is characterised by the following set of equalities

$$x(q, r) + e = s_y(p)$$
$$z(q, r) = z \tag{2.12}$$
$$L(q, r) = s_l(p) + l^z(z).$$

As to the nature of the numeraire in this economy, let us note that the supply functions (2.10) are homogeneous of degree zero in the producer price vector p, whereas the demand functions (2.8) are homogeneous of degree zero in (q, r^h), i.e. in both the consumer and the producer prices: indeed, r^h depends on p since, by (2.3), $r^h = \theta^h \pi = \theta^h p's$. Therefore multiplying both the consumer and the producer prices of an equilibrium price vector (p^*, q^*) by a positive constant does not affect the equilibrium. On the other hand, if the consumers did not hold shares in the private sector's profits, multiplying the producer prices only by a constant would also not affect the equilibrium. Therefore, and in other words, in models in which a 100 percent tax on profits is levied (or what amounts to the same, constant returns to scale prevail in the private sector), both one consumer and one producer price should be fixed in order to obtain a unique equilibrium tax vector (see Munk, 1978, for an exhaustive discussion of this point).

In our model however, since producer prices are arguments of the consumers' demand functions through profit shares, only one price (either a producer price or a consumer price) has to be fixed. Choosing the price of imports, as we have done, to play the role of numeraire amounts to fix foreign prices and exchange rates, which implies no loss of generality.

2.2.2 *Second-best optima*

For the economy that has just been described, we now assume that the public sector chooses the tax vector q in such a way as to maximise an additive social welfare function W over the set of equilibria defined by the equalities (2.12). Formally this behaviour may be described as the solution of the following problem

$$\begin{aligned} \operatorname*{Max}_q \; & W(q, r(q)) = \sum_h \mu^h V^h(q, r^h(q)) \\ \text{s.t.} \; & x(q, r) + e = s_y(p) \\ & z(q, r) \qquad = z \\ & L(q, r) \qquad = s_l(p) + l^z(z) \end{aligned} \tag{2.13}$$

where the μ^h's reflect distributive goals.

The allocation advocated by the solution to problem (2.13) must be achieved not only through a price vector q which makes the C^h's optimal from the consumers' point of view, but also through a vector p which is required to be such that the allocation is optimal for the producers. Finally the allocation should be technologically feasible, i.e. looking at (2.2′), (2.4) and (2.12) it should satisfy $L(q, r) = l^z(z) + l^p(y, m)$.

Now if we take a given equilibrium price vector q, we can easily show that a simple functional relationship exists between p and q. Indeed at equilibrium, we may use (2.12) to rewrite (2.11) as

$$\begin{aligned} p_{x_i}(q) &= \frac{\partial m}{\partial y_i}\{x(q, r(q)), L(q, r(q)) - l^z[z(q, r(q))]\}, \quad \forall i \\ p_l(q) &= \frac{\partial m}{\partial l}\{x(q, r(q)), L(q, r(q)) - l^z[z(q, r(q))]\} \end{aligned} \tag{2.14}$$

where the notation $r(q)$ makes use of the fact that profits depend, through p, x and L, on the consumer price vector q.

This last set of relations allows us, once we know q to be an equilibrium price vector, to find the vector p which makes the allocation optimal for the private producer.

The public sector's problem thus becomes to determine the optimal price system q under the sole feasibility constraint, i.e.

$$\begin{aligned} \operatorname*{Max}_q \; & W(q, r(q)) = \sum_h \mu^h V^h(q, r(q)) \\ \text{s.t.} \; & l^z(z) + l^p(y, m) = L(q, r(q)). \end{aligned} \tag{2.13′}$$

Adding the H consumers' budget constraints (1.1) one obtains

$$q_x' x(q, r) + q_z z(q, r) = q_l L(q, r) + \pi(q) \tag{2.15}$$

Substituting (2.3) and (2.13′) into (2.15) yields

$$\begin{aligned} q_x' x(q, r) + q_z z(q, r) = {} & q_l l^z(z) + q_l l^p(y, m) \\ & + p_x x(q, r) - p_l l^p(y, m) - B \end{aligned}$$

or,

$$(q_x - p_x)'x(.) + q_z z(.) + (p_l - q_l)l^p(y, m) - q_l l^z(z) - B = 0 \quad (2.16)$$

and this last expression is a mere re-statement of identity (2.6). The maximisation process can thus alternatively be carried out under a unique constraint bearing on the accounts of the public sector. However for the sake of comparison with results obtained in further sections we prefer not to incorporate the profit function in the social welfare function so that the problem to solve is the following

$$\begin{aligned} &\max_{(q,r^h)} W(q,r) = \sum_h \mu^h V^h(q, r^h) \quad (2.17)\\ &\text{s.t.} \quad S(q,r) = 0 \qquad (-\rho)\\ &\qquad r^h - \theta^h \pi(p) = 0 \qquad (-\sigma^h), \quad \forall h \end{aligned}$$

where ρ and the σ^h's are the Lagrange multipliers associated with the constraints.

Proposition 1

At the optimum of problem (2.17), there exists a vector and a scalar $\rho > 0$ such that

$$\sum_h \mu^h \varphi^h \left(C^h - \theta^h \frac{\partial \pi}{\partial q} \right) = \rho \left(\frac{\partial S}{\partial q} + \frac{\partial S}{\partial r} \frac{\partial \pi}{\partial q} \right) \quad (2.18)$$

where

$$\begin{aligned} \frac{\partial S}{\partial q} &= \frac{\partial x}{\partial q}(q_x - p_x) + \sum_h C^h + \frac{\partial x}{\partial q}(p_l - q_l)\frac{\partial l^p}{\partial y} \\ &\quad - \frac{\partial p_x}{\partial q} x + l^p \frac{\partial p_l}{\partial q} + (p_l - q_l)\frac{\partial l^{p'}}{\partial y}\frac{\partial x}{\partial r^h} \end{aligned}$$

$$\begin{aligned} \frac{\partial S}{\partial r} &= \sum_h \theta^h \frac{\partial S}{\partial r^h} \\ &= \sum_h \theta^h \bigg[(q_x - p_x)' \frac{\partial x}{\partial r^h} + (p_l - q_l)\frac{\partial l^{p'}}{\partial y}\frac{\partial x}{\partial r^h} \\ &\qquad + \left(q_z - q_l \frac{\partial l^z}{\partial z} \right) \frac{\partial z}{\partial r^h} - x' \frac{\partial p_x}{\partial r^h} + l^p \frac{\partial p_l}{\partial r^h} \bigg] \end{aligned}$$

$$\frac{\partial \pi}{\partial q} = \frac{\partial p_x}{\partial q} y - l^p \frac{\partial p_l}{\partial q} - \frac{\partial x}{\partial q}\frac{\partial m}{\partial y}$$

and $\dfrac{\partial x}{\partial q}$, $\dfrac{\partial p_x}{\partial q}$ are $(N + 2 \times N)$ matrices.

Proof At an optimum, the first derivatives of the Lagrangan of problem (2.17) read

$$\frac{\partial \Lambda}{\partial q} = \sum_h \mu^h \frac{\partial V^h}{\partial q} - \rho \frac{\partial S}{\partial q} + \sum_h \sigma^h \theta^h \frac{\partial \pi}{\partial q} = 0 \tag{2.19}$$

$$\frac{\partial \Lambda}{\partial r^h} = \sum_h \mu^h \frac{\partial V^h}{\partial r^h} - \rho \frac{\partial S}{\partial r^h} - \sigma^h = 0 \tag{2.19'}$$

We multiply each of the H equations (2.19′) by its corresponding θ^h and sum up to obtain

$$\sum_h \theta^h \mu^h \frac{\partial V^h}{\partial r^h} - \rho \sum_h \theta^h \frac{\partial S}{\partial r^h} - \sum_h \sigma^h \theta^h = 0 \tag{2.19''}$$

which may be simplified into

$$\sum_h \mu^h \theta^h \frac{\partial V^h}{\partial r^h} - \rho \frac{\partial S}{\partial r} - \sigma = 0 \tag{2.20}$$

where the new notational definitions are obvious.

(2.19) can also be written down as

$$\sum_h \mu^h \varphi^h C^h - \rho \frac{\partial S}{\partial q} - \sigma \frac{\partial \pi}{\partial q} = 0 \tag{2.21}$$

Substituting for σ from (2.20) into (2.21) yields

$$\sum_h \mu^h \varphi^h \left(C^h - \theta^h \frac{\partial \pi}{\partial q} \right) = \rho \left(\frac{\partial S}{\partial q} + \frac{\partial S}{\partial r} \frac{\partial \pi}{\partial q} \right).$$

Q.E.D.

Interpreted in terms of cost-benefit analysis, our second-best condition (2.18) states that at the optimum the marginal cost to households of an increase in q should be proportional to the marginal benefit accruing to the public sector from that very same increase in q. The left-hand side of (2.18) expresses the loss of utility incurred by the consumers when a variation dq takes place, whereas the right-hand side measures the impact of dq on the public sector's budget. Direct effects, i.e. $\frac{\partial S}{\partial q}$ and the actual consumption bundles C^h's, and derived effects emanating from the variations in profits, i.e. $\frac{\partial \pi}{\partial q}$, are taken into account. The multiplier ρ indicates the relative weights given to the consumers' welfare and to public finances.

Much intuitive insight as to the meaning of (2.18) is brought by the following argument. Denoting $\frac{\partial S}{\partial q_i}$ and $\frac{\partial W}{\partial q_i}$ the ith component of the right-hand side and left-hand side respectively of (2.18), the second-best condition is equivalent to

$$-\left(\frac{\partial W}{\partial q_i}\right)\left(\frac{\partial S}{\partial q_i}\right)^{-1} = -\left(\frac{\partial W}{\partial q_j}\right)\left(\frac{\partial S}{\partial q_j}\right)^{-1}, \quad \forall i, j \tag{2.18'}$$

$\left(\frac{\partial S}{\partial q_i}\right)^{-1}$ expresses the change in q_i necessary to yield an extra franc of revenue to the government; $-\left(\frac{\partial W}{\partial q_i}\right)\left(\frac{\partial S}{\partial q_i}\right)^{-1}$ denotes therefore the loss of social welfare induced by such a change. At equilibrium, the vector of taxes must be such that the loss of welfare induced by raising one franc of government income by adequate variation of each tax rate is equal. If the two sides of (2.18′) are not equal the government can increase total welfare by rearranging the tax rates. Assume, for example, that

$$-\left(\frac{\partial W}{\partial q_i}\right)\left(\frac{\partial S}{\partial q_i}\right)^{-1} < -\left(\frac{\partial W}{\partial q_j}\right)\left(\frac{\partial S}{\partial q_j}\right)^{-1},$$

then the government can improve welfare by decreasing q_i (which brings about a bigger increase in welfare than a decrease in q_j) and at the same time by decreasing q_j just enough to compensate for the fiscal loss due to the decrease in q_i. The government should therefore go on rearranging taxes along these lines until there is no further room to increase social welfare, i.e. until (2.18′) holds for all i's and j's.

This argument is, as we shall see in Chapter 3, at the basis of a process developed by Ahmad and Stern (1984) to determine desirable directions of tax reform.

A second important remark concerning the interpretation of (2.18) consists in observing that at the optimum the public sector must take account of producer price variations induced by tax changes. Indeed variation in consumer prices affect demand and thus profits, all of which go back to consumers and affects their welfare (through the term $\theta^h \frac{\partial \pi}{\partial q}$ in (2.18)). This result differs from the much celebrated conclusions of Diamond–Mirrlees (1971). In their model, constant returns to scale (which is equivalent to a 100 percent tax on profits) are assumed to prevail. This no pure profit assumption guarantees that the tax variations affect households only qua consumers and not qua asset holders. It also follows that at the optimum both private and public sectors maximise the value of production in terms of producer prices and that aggregate productive efficiency is desirable.

As shown by Dasgupta and Stiglitz (1972), once some constraint is imposed on the taxation power of the government, which is the case in our model as profits cannot be taxed, the shadow prices in the public production sector need not be equal to producer prices so that productive efficiency is no longer a desirable property of the optimum.

The computation of tax rates satisfying relations of type (2.18) requires the use of fixed-point algorithms but these seem to be quite deceptive. For instance Harris and Mackinnon (1979) conclude that '... optimal tax rates are exceedingly sensitive to the specification of the model used to derive them'. Such algorithms also require the constant revision of the matrix of price elasticities and of the vector of the marginal propensities to consume: this delicate process may lead to unreliable results. Finally knowledge of the optimal tax vector could be useless for practical purposes as 'actual changes are slow and piecemeal' (Feldstein, 1975). These considerations have led economists to look for methods defining 'small' tax moves that increase utility without affecting the balance of the public sector. This new approach – not new it seems to the field of international economics (e.g. Negishi, 1971) – has been introduced into the public finance literature by Dixit (1975) and Guesnerie (1977) under the name of 'tax reform'. Although this topic and that of second-best theory are closely related, philosophy and techniques differ greatly between the two subjects. As we shall now see, second-best singles out one solution which might be 'far away' from the prevailing tax vector whereas tax reform may leave the decision taker with a whole set of possibilities to choose from.

2.2.3 Tax reform problem

Two types of reform can be considered:

1 *A collectively improving tax reform* (*CITR*)

One seeks price variations which increase the weighted sum of the agents' utilities as expressed in (2.17) and which leave the public sector's budget unaffected. In this case it may be that only a few agents benefit from the reform while the other agents' utility is in fact decreased.

2 *A Pareto improving tax reform* (*PITR*)

One is looking for tax moves which improve every agent's utility, whatever positive weight μ^h is attributed in (2.17) to each individual. This kind of reform is also called 'Pareto Improving Tax Reform' (see Guesnerie, 1977).

Before computing actual directions of such moves, our first task consists in defining their conditions of existence. The analysis of algorithms checking whether these conditions of existence obtain for a particular economy is discussed in Chapter 3.

First of all, let us adopt the following notation

$$(\partial V^h) = \frac{\partial V^h}{\partial q} + \frac{\partial V^h}{\partial r^h} \theta^h \frac{\partial \pi}{\partial q} \tag{2.22}$$

or equivalently by (2.8)–(2.9)

$$(\partial C^h) = \varphi^h \left(C^h - \theta^h \frac{\partial \pi}{\partial q} \right) \tag{2.22'}$$

with $(\partial C^h) = \frac{-1}{\varphi^h} (\partial V^h)$.

Equation (2.22) expresses the incidence of a variation dq on the agents' utility whereas (2.22′) does the same but expresses this impact in terms of quantities consumed and of profit shares.

We also define

$$(\partial S) = \frac{\partial S}{\partial q} + \frac{\partial S}{\partial r} \frac{\partial \pi}{\partial q}. \tag{2.23}$$

(∂S) reflects the incidence on the public sector's accounts of a variation dq.

In view of (2.22′) and (2.23) let us note that the second-best optimum condition may now be reformulated as

$$\sum_h \lambda^h (\partial C^h) = (\partial S)$$

where $\lambda^h = \frac{\mu^h \varphi^h}{\rho}$.

1 *CITR*

We must find dq's improving a social welfare function which is linear in every agent's utility and associates to each such utility a weight that is arbitrarily fixed by the decision taker. That is, find dq such that for given λ^h's

$$\sum_h \lambda^h (\partial V^h)' dq \geqslant 0 \tag{2.24}$$

or

$$\sum_h \lambda^h (\partial C^h)' dq \leqslant 0. \tag{2.24'}$$

On the other hand the price variations must leave the public sector's accounts unaffected, i.e.

$$(\partial S)'dq = 0. \tag{2.25}$$

It is quite obvious that as long as the two vectors $\sum_h \lambda^h(\partial V^h)$ and (∂S) are not collinear, there will exist at least one direction dq which improves welfare without perturbing S. The collinearity of the two vectors would mean that the economy is already at a second-best optimum for the *a priori* fixed λ^h's (i.e. equation (2.18) obtains). As noted by Drèze (1984) an easy way to determine an improving direction in this case is to select a dq in the orthogonal hyperplane to (∂S) and check whether (2.24) obtains. If not, $(-dq)$ is an eligible tax reform movement.

2 *PITR*

We are now looking for tax directions dq such that

$$(\partial C^h)'dq \leqslant 0, \quad \forall h \tag{2.26}$$

and

$$(\partial S)'dq = 0. \tag{2.26'}$$

The problem may equivalently be formulated as follows: what are the conditions of existence of tax directions which increase every agent's utility, whatever the positive weight attributed to each individual in the social welfare function, and which at the same time leave the accounts of the public sector unaffected. Using Guesnerie's terminology, the tax moves associated with such a reform are labelled 'Pareto Improving Directions' (PID).

In order to assess the conditions of existence of PID we introduce the following sets: Λ, Λ^* and $S^{\perp}$.

$$\Lambda = [\lambda | \lambda = \sum_h (\partial C^h), \lambda^h \geqslant 0] \tag{2.7}$$

Λ is the cone generated by the vectors characterising each agent's situation in terms of consumption and of profit sharing. Since $(\partial C^h) = \dfrac{-1}{\varphi^h}(\partial V^h)$, one could also interpret Λ as the opposite of the cone generated by the agents' marginal utilities.

$$\Lambda^* = [dq | \lambda' dq \leqslant 0, \lambda \in \Lambda]. \tag{2.28}$$

Intuitively Λ^* is the set of consumer price directions which decrease the cost of the consumption bundles or, in other words, which increase the agents' marginal utilities. In more technical terms, Λ^* is called the positive polar cone of Λ. We also define the interior of Λ^* as

$$\mathring{\Lambda} = [dq \mid \lambda' dq < 0, \lambda \in \Lambda]. \tag{2.28'}$$

Finally

$$S^{\perp} = [dq \mid (\partial S)' dq = 0]. \tag{2.29}$$

$S^{\perp}$ is the set of tax directions which leave the budget of the public sector unchanged and is thus the orthogonal hyperplane to (∂S).

As shown in Proposition 2, the existence of PID's respecting (2.26′) depends exclusively on the position of (∂S) with respect to Λ.

Proposition 2

(i) There exist no PID respecting (2.26′) if $(\partial S) \in \Lambda$.

(ii) PID's exist at the cost of inefficiencies if $(\partial S) \in -\Lambda$.

(iii) There exist PID's respecting (2.26′) if $(\partial S) \in \complement(\Lambda \cup -\Lambda)$.

The proof of Proposition 2 is similar to that provided by Guesnerie (1977, p. 190) and will not therefore be reproduced here. We may however examine the three cases in a more intuitive fashion.

(i) $(\partial S) \in \Lambda$

As can be seen in the following illustration, which characterises a two-agents, two-goods economy, $S^{\perp} \cap \mathring{\Lambda}^* = \phi$, i.e. there is no direction which respects (2.26′) and which is, at the same time, included in $\mathring{\Lambda}^*$.

This is easily understandable as, in this case, the economy is already at a second-best optimum for a certain set of weights $\tilde{\lambda}^h$'s. Indeed

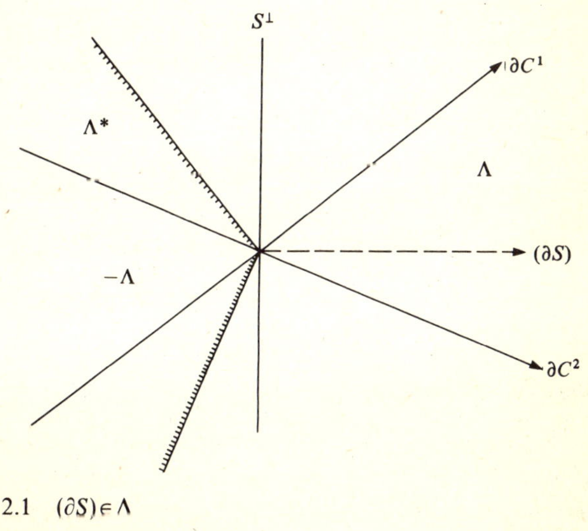

Figure 2.1 $(\partial S) \in \Lambda$

$(\partial S) \in -\Lambda$ is equivalent to saying that $(\exists \tilde{\lambda}^h)$: $\sum_h \tilde{\lambda}^h(\partial C^h) = (\partial S)$ which characterises a second-best optimum (see (2.18)). As is clearly seen in our illustration, (∂S) may be written as a positive linear combination of ∂C^1 and ∂C^2.

(ii) $(\partial S) \in -\Lambda$

In this case we also have $S^{\perp} \cap \mathring{\Lambda}^* = \phi$ but on the other hand the economy is not at a second-best optimum since $\nexists \tilde{\lambda}^h \geqslant 0$: $\sum_h \tilde{\lambda}^h(\partial C)^h = (\partial S)$. The only way to 'unblock' this situation would be to implement a tax direction included in Λ^* but which increases at the same time the public sector surplus, i.e. find $\tilde{d}q \in \Lambda^*$ such that $(\partial S)'\tilde{d}q > 0$. Adopting such a direction would thus imply that, temporarily, the public sector accumulates a surplus which will not be redistributed to the agents (see Figure 2.2).

(iii) $(\partial S) \in \complement\,(\Lambda \cup -\Lambda)$

From Figure 2.3, we can immediately see that $S^{\perp} \cap \mathring{\Lambda}^* \neq \phi$. In this case, one can find tax directions which increase each agent's utility whilst leaving unaffected the public sector's finances. It is obvious that in this situation one could also choose Pareto improving directions creating, as in the previous case, a surplus in the public sector finances. As will be seen in Chapter 5, this latter possibility should not be neglected by the decision maker.

One of the main advantages of the procedure presented above lies in the relative ease with which one can empirically verify the conditions of existence of a PITR. The public sector needs to know the consumption bundles of the consumers, the matrix of partial derivatives of consumption

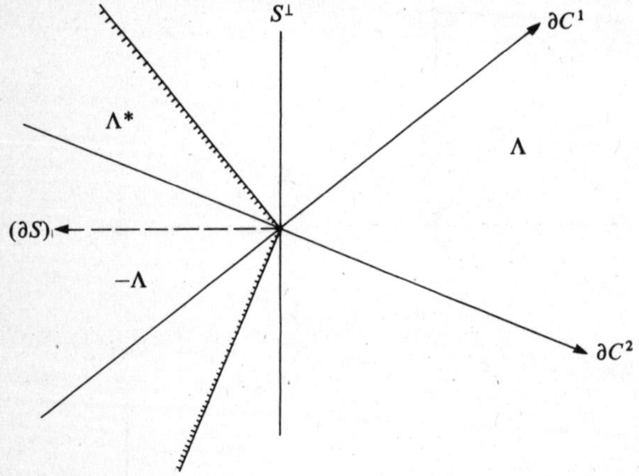

Figure 2.2 $(\partial S) \in -\Lambda$

with respect to prices and income and finally the distribution of profits amongst the agents. It is noteworthy that we do not need to know the individual elasticities of demand, and that an estimate of the matrix of elasticities of aggregate demand suffices. If the conditions of existence are satisfied, one can look for Pareto improving directions increasing the value of the social welfare function associated with a certain set of $\tilde{\lambda}^{h'} \geqslant 0$, knowing that these directions will also increase all the other positive linear combinations of the agents' utilities.

The above analysis allows the decision taker to choose an improving direction, if one exists, out of a whole set of possible moves. Two remarks should however be made about the probability of finding PID's. First, the bigger the cone Λ is, the greater the chances are of having $(\partial S) \in \Lambda$ or $(\partial S) \in (-\Lambda)$, i.e. of not finding PID's. The size of Λ actually depends on the position of its generating vectors and will thus be larger if the latter differ widely from one another or, in other words, if the economy is characterised by considerable inequalities between households. In this, the geometry of the tax reform problem only corroborates our intuition which tells us that a PITR will be more difficult to implement if we attempt to satisfy people who are very different from one another. This argument also tends to support the idea that the wider the distribution of income, the greater the chances of society being at a Pareto optimum.

Secondly, and as has already been observed by Guesnerie (1977, p. 194), the requirement for an improving tax reform direction to belong to $S^{\perp}$ only removes one degree of freedom for the possible movements dq. This constraint implies that, if the number of consumers is less than or equal

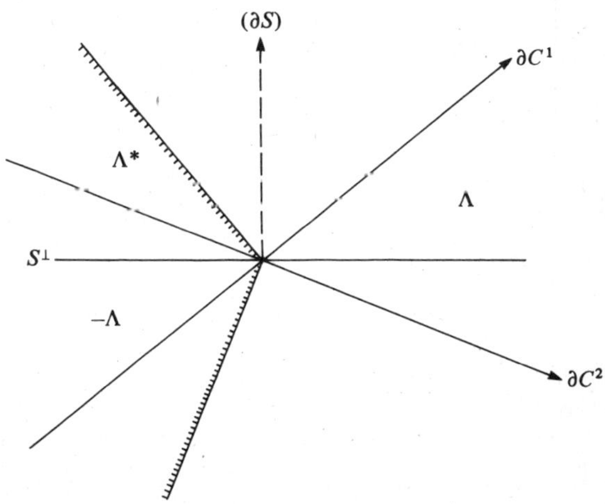

Figure 2.3 $(\partial S) \in \complement(\Lambda \cup -\Lambda)$

to the number of commodities minus two, the sets Λ and $(-\Lambda)$ will be of measure zero with respect to the hyperplane Λ^*. In this situation, the probability of having $(\partial S) \in \Lambda$ or $(\partial S) \in (-\Lambda)$ will therefore tend to zero, or in other words, the probability of finding PID's will almost certainly be equal to one.

These remarks suggest that when one tries to verify empirically whether the conditions of existence of PID's obtain in a particular economy, one should be very careful when aggregating the consumption data and selecting representative individuals,[1] since the results of the whole analysis could be rendered devoid of meaning by a poor choice of these data.

As mentioned above, second-best results can be interpreted in terms of cost-benefit analysis. In the same vein, Diewert (1983) and Hammond (1986) try to figure out under what conditions 'small' tax movements could accompany a 'small' government project in order to provide society with a Pareto gain.

Their approach is totally identical to that of tax reform and relies on the observation that the traditional cost-benefit literature is concerned with 'large' projects for which global information about preferences and technology is required. On the other hand real-world projects are often small – or even infinitesimal – with respect to a national economy; for these projects only local information should be considered.

The test for a favourable project as advocated by Diewert and Hammond is not whether it produces a Paretian improvement directly but whether the adoption of the project can be followed by a tax reform so that the combined effects of the project and of the reform are welfare improving. As noted by Hammond, this kind of evaluation becomes inevitable since the introduction of the project, even if directly welfare improving, may cause a public sector budget imbalance which will have to be corrected somehow, for instance by a tax reform.

The economy Diewert and Hammond are concerned with is of the small and open type and is characterised by constant returns to scale (no pure profits) in the production sector and a constraint on its balance of trade. Without entering into technical details, a small project can be viewed as a step in a certain direction of the commodity space. Diewert and Hammond look for the conditions under which there exists a half space of directions such that any project included in this half space can be followed by a tax reform in order to yield a Pareto improvement. These existence conditions are derived for the different sets of instruments at hand: consumption taxes, lump-sum transfers, and taxes on traded goods.

[1] We suppose here that some kind of aggregation on the commodities will be needed to estimate the price- and income-elasticities and that the decision maker cannot realistically possess information on all individuals.

The shadow price at which the project should be evaluated is simply the normal to the hyperplane bounding the half space of project directions. Indeed the commodity space is partitioned into two half spaces separated by a hyperplane whose normal is the shadow-price vector: acceptable directions lie on one side of the separating hyperplane, those to be rejected lie on the other side. This expresses the standard idea that projects, evaluated at appropriately chosen shadow prices, should be undertaken only if their net value is positive.

In this respect, a major concern in Diewert's and Hammond's papers is the border pricing rule whereby prices for traded goods are proportional to world prices (see Little and Mirrlees, 1974). This question has been studied in depth by Mookherjee (1986) for the case of small projects and he concludes that the border pricing rule is particularly sensitive to '. . . the assumption that the reaction of the instruments to a proposed project depends on the tradeable components of that project only through its foreign exchange value' (p. 304). One important implication of this is that the border pricing rule does not apply to the case of a private sector project generating profits which are distributed to households or to a public sector project generating price movements which affect demand and profits. In these cases, the variations in profits will have an impact on the utility and the demand of some households. This, in turn, will affect the public sector balance in a way which will not depend on the foreign exchange value of the tradeable component of the initial project. This situation is quite akin to what we are dealing with in this book. We can therefore conclude that the border pricing rule does not apply to our model and this conclusion, as we shall see later, is but reinforced once quantity rationing enters the picture.

A criticism to the Diewert–Hammond approach, which was raised by Hammond himself, consists in the danger of accepting an otherwise uneconomical project because it is accompanied by a favourable tax reform. Needless to say that, if such a situation was to occur, it would be better to discard the project altogether and keep the reform. This cannot happen in our approach since the price – and hence quantity – of the public production Z is not privileged in any way so that the reform advocated must be accepted in full. If one part of the tax reform is discarded then either welfare will decrease or the public sector balance will be disrupted (or both). However our reform may bring about a decrease in the production of commodity Z which cannot happen in the Diewert–Hammond framework. This only reflects the main difference between the two approaches: they want to determine the best way to finance a project in order to bring an overall Pareto improvement whereas we seek a 'better' consumer price vector irrespective of what happens in the public production sector. In this respect, our problem has less constraints.

We are also convinced that disequilibrium considerations should be incorporated in the Diewert–Hammond analysis. Developing countrys' economies are the natural field for application of public project evaluation. Such societies, afflicted as they are with price rigidities and quantity rationing, can hardly be considered as the archetypes of the Walrasian system. Precise formulae for shadow prices, and wages taking account of the quantity constraints, must therefore be designed and used for the evaluation of projects in non-Walrasian contexts. As we shall see later several contributions already exist in this respect but this avenue is still wide open for further research.

2.3 The Keynesian case

2.3.1 Introduction

In this section and the two following ones, we investigate the second-best and tax reform problems for economies in so-called 'disequilibrium'.

These economies are characterised by the existence of rationed agents, i.e. agents who at the going prices cannot fulfil their buying or selling plans. One obvious manifestation of rationing is involuntary unemployment. Once the existence of such a phenomenon is admitted then it becomes quite natural to wonder how rationing may occur on the markets. One answer which has become more and more popular among the economists is that of the so-called 'fix-price' theory according to which – and contrary to classical teaching – prices are sticky or exogeneously fixed in the short run, so that markets do not clear through price adjustments but through quantity adjustments. Given the short-run price stickiness, it is therefore justified to assume full price- and wage-rigidity; this assumption has become one of the main features of the ill-named 'disequilibrium theory'.

It is not our objective to survey all the contributions to disequilibrium theory for this would bring us too far away from our main topic. However the way several authors justify – theoretically and empirically – the fixed-price assumption is deserving of our attention.

After the seminal contributions of Clower (1965) and Leijonhufvud (1968), who introduced the concept of quantity adjustment, one line of research consisted of studying macroeconomic issues – essentially unemployment – starting from specific aggregated models. Some well-known papers and books in this area are: Barro and Grossman (1971), Benassy (1973), Malinvaud (1977), and Muellbauer and Portes (1978).

A second line of research based on the microeconomic foundations of disequilibrium theory, studies how quantity adjustments take place on the markets once the hypothesis of price flexibility is abandoned: see, e.g.

Drèze (1975, Benassy (1975, 1976), Malinvaud and Younes (1978), and Younes (1975).

None of these authors gives an explanation to the price rigidity apart from the factual observation that although quick price adjustments do take place on some markets (those for raw materials essentially), nothing of the kind happens on the markets for manufactured goods, services or labour. On these markets excess demands or supplies exist and take the form of delivery dates, excess capacities, and unemployment.

In this respect the price rigidity may be due to institutional constraints such as minimum wage legislation or government controlled price commissions which are a common feature in Western Europe (not to speak about price controls in socialist economies and developing countries). Another reason which is frequently invoked is that the price stickiness results from rational behaviour. Economic agents face uncertainty and transaction costs which may induce them to react, in the short run, in terms of quantities rather than in terms of prices. In this context, Baily's paper (1974) provided a first formalisation and gave rise to several contributions (see Azariadis and Stiglitz, 1983); one can be pretty sure that the resources of this approach are far from being totally exhausted today.

Another way of explaining price stickiness lies in the existence of imperfect or monopolistic competition. Contributions in this field are still relatively few (the main ones being probably Benassy, 1976 and Hart, 1982) as, not surprisingly, the same technical difficulties in proving the existence of an imperfect competition equilibrium in a flexible price context are also encountered in the quantity rationing framework. Since in this book perfect competition is assumed to prevail, we shall not comment on this line of research any further.

Beside the theoretical contributions, there is now a whole part of the econometric literature which substantiates the relevancy of the fixed-price approach. For example, models explaining price variations by a fixed mark-up factor over costs fit the data quite well (see, for instance, Drèze and Sneessens, 1986). Limiting ourselves to econometric models relevant to the Belgian economy, the estimations carried out by Sneessens (1981) and Lambert (1986) yield an excellent approximation to the evolution of output and unemployment during the last quarter of century.

Finally a recent paper by Carlton (1986) investigates how rigid prices are, using data on individual transaction prices (not price indices) in several industrial sectors of the U.S. economy. Carlton's main conclusion is that in many industries the degree of price rigidity is significant. Defining the average duration of price rigidity as the average number of months for which prices remain unchanged, Carlton finds that out of the thirty-two commodities he analysed most of them have an average duration of price rigidity in excess of eight months. It is not even unusual for some prices to remain unchanged for two years. Carlton therefore concludes that '. . . non-price rationing is not a fiction, it is a reality of business and may be the efficient response to economic uncertainty and the cost of using the price system' (p. 638).

We make his our conclusions.

During the last few years several authors have studied what the impact of the 'fixed-price' assumption could be on the theory of public finance: e.g. Dixit (1976) studies the effect of tax variations on an economy in Keynesian disequilibrium, Bronsard and Wagneur (1980) present second-best optima in fixed-price models stressing the comparative statics aspects, Picard (1981) examines optima for disequilibrium economies subject to constraints on their public and international balance, and Drèze (1984) applies the Boiteux model to an economy in a Keynesian regime and then links, through second-best solutions, micro and macro theories of fixed-price models.

Our purpose is to study the second-best and tax reform problems for the model presented in the previous sections but supposing alternatively a Keynesian or a classical disequilibrium (in this section and in the next one respectively). We also study an intermediate case in which unemployment is observed but cannot be attributed to either the Keynesian or the classical regime. This situation, which we call the 'uncertainty case', is to be examined in Section 2.5. Finally, in Section 2.6, the case in which some agents are rationed Keynesian-wise and others classical-wise is taken up. Let us now turn our attention to the pure Keynesian case.

2.3.2 The agents and the markets

The consumers are now constrained on the labour market since firms, which are facing a slackness in the aggregate demand, cannot match the labour supply. More formally agent h's labour supply is subject to the following constraint: $l^h = \bar{l}^h(L)$ where L is the total employment in the economy. It is assumed that $\sum_h \partial\bar{l}^h/\partial L = 1$ which reflects the fact that an increase in the labour demand is always met by the agents' supply. It is also assumed that the latter is locally inelastic to all prices.

Each agent receives now from the public sector an unemployment allowance equal to $a(l^* - \bar{l}^h)$ where l^* is the full employment level. We therefore redefine r^h as $r^h = \theta^h\pi + a(l^* - \bar{l}^h)$.

Agent h maximises hence his utility under a budget and a labour-rationing constraint

$$\text{Max } u^h(C^h), \quad \forall h \tag{2.30}$$

$$\text{s.t.} \quad q'C^h = r^h \quad (-\varphi^h)$$

$$e^h = \bar{l}^h \quad (-\psi^h)$$

where φ^h and ψ^h are the Lagrange multipliers associated with the constraints.

The maximisation of (2.30) yields the following relations

$$\begin{aligned} l^h &= \bar{l}^h(L) \\ x^h &= x^h(q, r^h, \bar{l}^h) \qquad (2.31) \\ z^h &= z^h(q, r^h, \bar{l}^h) \end{aligned}$$

where one notes the appearance of the spill-over effect of the labour market on the demand for goods.

The excess supply of labour is characterised by

$$-\frac{\partial u^h}{\partial l^h} < \varphi^h q_l, \quad \forall h \qquad (2.32)$$

In Appendix 1, we show that in terms of the indirect utility function $V^h(q, r^h, \bar{l}^h)$ one obtains

$$\frac{\partial V^h}{\partial q} = -\varphi^h C^h, \qquad \frac{\partial V^h}{\partial r^h} = \varphi^h \quad \text{and} \quad \frac{\partial V^h}{\partial \bar{l}} = \psi^h. \qquad (2.33)$$

The private sector still maximises its profits (2.3) under the technological constraint (2.2). However it now faces an additional constraint as its sales cannot exceed a level $\bar{y}_i$ equal to the sum of exports and of the agents' global consumption $x_i = \sum_h x_i^h(.)$ (for $i = 1, \ldots, N$). Thus we have

$$\begin{aligned} &\text{Max } \pi = p_x' y - p_l l^p - m \qquad (2.34) \\ &\text{s.t.} \quad y = y(l^p, m) \\ &\qquad \bar{y} = e + \sum_h x^h(q, r^h, \bar{l}^h) \quad (-\xi). \end{aligned}$$

The equilibrium of the private sector is now characterised by

$$(p_{x_i} - \xi_i)\frac{\partial y_i}{\partial l^p} = p_l \quad \text{and} \quad (p_{x_i} - \xi_i)\frac{\partial y_i}{\partial m} = 1, \quad \forall i.$$

Demand for inputs takes the form

$$l^p = l^p(p, \bar{y}) \quad \text{and} \quad m = m(p, \bar{y}). \qquad (2.35)$$

As p_x, p_l and e are exogeneously fixed we shall hereafter note $l^p = l^p(y) = l^p(x)$ and $m = m(x)$.

The excess supply of y is characterised by

$$p_l \frac{\partial l^p}{\partial y_i} \leqslant p_{x_i} \quad \text{and} \quad \frac{\partial m}{\partial y_i} \leqslant p_{x_i},$$

i.e. the price of the output is higher than its marginal cost.

The public sector still collects taxes on x and l and sells good Z; its accounts write now as

$$S(q, r, L) = (q_x - p_x)'x(.) + q_z z(.) + (p_l - q_l)l^p(x) \\ - q_l l^z(z) - a(L^* - L) \qquad (2.36)$$

where $L^* = Hl^*$.

Comparing the public sector's accounts in the Keynesian and the Walrasian contexts (see (2.5)), we note that the only difference between the two formulations lies in the presence in the former of the unemployment constraint. This constraint appears explicitly in (2.36) through the term $a(L^* - L)$ and indirectly as an argument of the demand functions $x(.)$ and $z(.)$.

2.3.3 Second-best optima

Following Drèze (1984) who deals with a similar model the public sector's decisions are the solution of the following problem

$$\max_{(q, r^h, l)} W(q, r, L) = \sum_h \mu^h V^h(q, r^h, \bar{l}^h) \qquad (2.37)$$

$$\text{s.t.} \quad L - l^z(z) - l^p(x) = 0 \qquad (-\nu)$$

$$r^h - a(l^* - \bar{l}^h) - \theta^h \pi = 0 \qquad (-\sigma^h), \quad \forall h$$

$$S(q, r, L) = 0 \qquad (\rho)$$

The constraints appertaining to non-labour income and to the rationing on the labour market may have been incorporated in the objective function. However we prefer to adopt formulation (2.37) since it yields readily interpretable results.

Proposition 3

First-order conditions for obtaining an optimum to problem (2.37) require the decision taker to find a vector dq and a scalar $\rho > 0$ such that

$$\rho\left(\frac{\partial S}{\partial q} + \frac{\partial S}{\partial r}\frac{\partial \pi}{dq} + \frac{\partial S}{\partial L}\frac{dL}{dq}\right) \\ = \sum_h \mu^h \left[C^h - \theta^h \frac{d\pi}{dq} - (q_l - a - q_R^h)\frac{dl^h}{dq}\right] \qquad (2.38)$$

where

$$\frac{\partial S}{\partial q} = \sum_h C^h + \frac{\partial x}{\partial q}(q_x - p_x) + \frac{\partial x}{\partial q}(p_l - q_l)\frac{\partial l^p}{\partial x} \\ + \left(q_z - q_l\frac{\partial l^z}{\partial z}\right)\frac{\partial z}{\partial q} + a\frac{\partial L}{\partial q}$$

$$\frac{\partial S}{\partial r}=\sum_h \theta^h \frac{\partial S}{\partial r^h}=\sum_h \theta^h\Bigg[(q_x-p_x)'\frac{\partial x}{\partial r^h}+(p_l-q_l)\frac{\partial l^{p\prime}}{\partial x}\frac{\partial x}{\partial r^h}$$

$$+\left(q_z-q_l\frac{\partial l^z}{\partial z}\right)\frac{\partial z}{\partial r^h}+a\frac{\partial L}{\partial r^h}\Bigg]$$

$$\frac{\partial S}{\partial l}=(q_x-p_x)'\frac{\partial x}{\partial l}+(p_l-q_l)\frac{\partial l^{p\prime}}{\partial x}\frac{\partial x}{\partial l}$$

$$+\left(q_z-q_l\frac{\partial l^z}{\partial z}\right)\frac{\partial z}{\partial l}+a\frac{\partial L}{\partial l}$$

$$\begin{pmatrix}\dfrac{d\pi}{dq}\\[2mm] \dfrac{dL}{dq}\end{pmatrix}=\begin{pmatrix}\dfrac{\partial\pi}{\partial q} & \dfrac{\partial L}{\partial q}\end{pmatrix}\cdot\begin{pmatrix}-\left(\dfrac{\partial l^{p\prime}}{\partial x}\dfrac{\partial x}{\partial r}+\dfrac{\partial l^z}{\partial z}\dfrac{\partial z}{\partial r}\right) & 1-\dfrac{\partial\pi}{\partial r}\\[2mm] \left(1-\dfrac{\partial l^p}{\partial x}\dfrac{\partial x}{\partial l}-\dfrac{\partial l^z}{\partial z}\dfrac{\partial z}{\partial l}\right) & -\dfrac{\partial\pi}{\partial L}\end{pmatrix}^{-1}$$

with

$$\frac{\partial L}{\partial q}=\frac{\partial x}{\partial q}\frac{\partial l^p}{\partial x}+\frac{\partial l^z}{\partial z}\frac{\partial z}{\partial q}$$

$$\frac{\partial L}{\partial \gamma}=\frac{\partial l^{p\prime}}{\partial x}\frac{\partial x}{\partial \gamma}+\frac{\partial l^z}{\partial z}\frac{\partial z}{\partial \gamma}\quad \text{for } \gamma=(r^h, l)$$

$$\frac{\partial \pi}{\partial \tau}=\left(p_x-p_l\frac{\partial l^p}{\partial x}\right)'\frac{\partial x}{\partial \tau}\quad \text{for } \tau=(q, r^h, l)$$

and, finally, q_R^h is agent h's reservation wage.

The proof of Proposition 3 can be found in Appendix 2.

As in the Walrasian case, a cost-benefit analysis interpretation can be given to formula (2.38). Indeed, the marginal cost to the households of an increase in q must be proportional to the marginal benefit to the public sector. However there are differences in the way costs and revenues are evaluated since, in a Keynesian context, these consist of three parts, instead of two as in the Walrasian case. Indeed a change in the tax vector affects each household in its being a consumer (C^h), an asset holder ($\theta^h d\pi/dq$) and a constrained labour supplier ($(q_l-q_R^h)dl^h/dq$). Now if a tax increase has a negative effect on employment ($dL/dq<0$), each household suffers a loss of welfare equal to the difference between the market wage and its reservation wage, multiplied by the change in the labour constraint. In the Walrasian model this third impact does not appear as the reservation wage equals the market wage.

A second difference with respect to the Walrasian case lies in the way the impact of a change in q on profits ($d\pi/dq$) is computed. This leads us quite naturally to comment on the nature of the multipliers $d\pi/dq$ and dL/dq.

When a tax increase dq_i takes place, households adjust their demand by an amount given by the price derivative $\partial X/\partial q_i$. These changes in demand affect profits and labour through the terms $\partial\pi/\partial q_i$ and $\partial L/\partial q_i$ respectively. Variations in profits and labour affect households consumption (through $\partial\pi/\partial r^h$, $\partial\pi/\partial \mathrm{l}$, $\partial L/\partial r^h$ and $\partial L/\partial \mathrm{l}$) and so on. The Keynesian text book multiplier process operates and yields the final impact on profits and employment, i.e. $d\pi/dq$ and dL/dq respectively.

These results are a generalisation of those obtained by Drèze (1984), for the problem of the pricing rules of a public sector subject to a budget constraint. They also encompass those obtained by Johansson (1982) in his attempt to derive cost-benefit rules for project evaluation in disequilibrium economies. Taxes are however absent in both these papers. In Johansson's paper in particular, any surplus or deficit of the public sector accounts accruing from the adoption of a project is disposed of by lump-sum transfers. The main question in this paper is really how welfare is affected when the government varies the size of the project and in this respect our results are quite similar to Johansson's: when manipulating the instruments at hand (prices or quantities), the government ought to take account of profit- and of employment multipliers and of reservation wages. Once we get rid of the unrealistic assumption of lump-sum transfers, it becomes necessary however to determine what taxing rule the government should adopt to finance the project and how that rule will affect welfare. Therefore (2.38) can be thought of as the condition to be met by the government when it is looking simultaneously for the optimal size of the project (Z) and the optimal consumption price vector (q).

In summary, the second-best conditions characterising a Walrasian and a Keynesian economy can both be interpreted in cost-benefit analysis terms, i.e. there must be at the optimum proportionality between the marginal costs to the agents and the marginal benefits to the public sector. However the two sets of conditions depart from one another in the way costs and benefits are computed. Depending on how markets clear in the short run, through prices or through quantity rationing, the policy maker has to get hold of very different pieces of information. In the Walrasian case he should reckon how production prices react to changes in consumption taxes and how these production price variations affect the private sector's profits. In a Keynesian economy, he should not bother about production prices but estimate how employment and production are affected by consumer price variations. He should also estimate, and this might be more troublesome, the reservation wages q_R^h's, i.e. the wage at which an unemployed agent is ready to work. These quantities are unobservable and will typically vary from one agent to another. However sample surveys may be used to estimate them or simulations using several 'plausible' values of the q_R^h's may be carried out to compute a second-best tax vector.

2.3.4 *Tax reform problem*

Before analysing the tax reform problem in the Keynesian case, let us adopt the following notation

$$(\partial V_K^h) = \frac{\partial V^h}{\partial q} + \theta^h \varphi^h \frac{d\pi}{dq} + \psi^h \frac{dl^h}{dq} \tag{2.39}$$

or equivalently

$$(\partial C_K^h) = C^h - \theta^h \frac{d\pi}{dq} - (q_l - a - q_R^h) \frac{dl^h}{dq} \tag{2.40}$$

with $(\partial C_K^h) = -\frac{1}{\varphi^h}(\partial V_K^h)$

$$(\partial S_K) = \frac{\partial S}{\partial q} + \frac{\partial S}{\partial r}\frac{d\pi}{dq} + \frac{\partial S}{\partial L}\frac{dL}{dq} \tag{2.41}$$

Equations (2.39) and (2.41) express the global incidence of dq on the agents' utilities and on the public finances respectively.

It turns out that the conditions of existence of CITR and PITR are similar to those displayed in the Walrasian case. Indeed for the CITR we look for dq's such that for given $\bar{\lambda}^h$'s

$$\sum_h \bar{\lambda}^h (\partial C_K^h)' dq \leqslant 0$$

and $\quad (\partial S_K)' dq = 0.$

Such dq's will always exist as long as the economy is not at a second-best optimum for the particular set of $\bar{\lambda}^h$'s.

For the PITR we have to define

$$\Lambda_K = [\lambda_K | \lambda_K = \sum \lambda^h (\partial C_K^h), \lambda^h \geqslant 0] \tag{2.42}$$

$$\mathring{\Lambda}_K^* = [dq | \lambda_K' dq < 0, \forall \lambda_K \in \Lambda_K] \tag{2.43}$$

$$S_K^{\perp} = [dq \,|\, (\partial S_K)' dq = 0]. \tag{2.44}$$

The interpretation to be given to these sets is identical to that proposed for (Λ, Λ^*, $S^{\perp}$) in the Walrasian case and will not therefore be reproduced here.

A necessary condition of existence of PID's is again

$$(\partial S_K) \in \complement\,(\Lambda_K \cup -\Lambda_K). \tag{2.45}$$

We shall not go through all the steps of the interpretation of the three cases $(\partial S_K) \in \Lambda_K$, $(\partial S_K) \in -\Lambda_K$ and $(\partial S_K) \in \complement\,(\Lambda_K \cup -\Lambda_K)$. The comments are of the same type as those given for the Walrasian case but for one point: in order to check whether the conditions of existence of PITR are fulfilled, and besides getting knowledge of the consumption bundles and of the matrix of price elasticities, the government should also estimate the global substitution effect between labour and consumption and the reservation wage of each agent (see (2.40)).

2.4 The classical case

2.4.1 The agents' equilibrium

Each agent is now rationed on the labour market but also on the markets for the goods produced by the private sector. Household h faces the following quantity constraints

$$l^h = \bar{l}^h(L)$$

$$x_i^h = \bar{x}_i^h(y_i), \quad i = 1, \ldots, N$$

where y_i is the aggregate production of good i. It is also assumed that $\sum_h \frac{\partial \bar{l}^h}{\partial L} = 1 = \sum_h \frac{\partial \bar{x}_i^h}{\partial y_i}$ $(i = 1, \ldots, N)$. Each agent maximises his utility under $N+2$ **constraints**

$$\text{Max } u^u(C^h) \tag{2.46}$$

$$\text{s.t.} \quad q,\, C^h = r^h \quad (-\varphi^h)$$

$$l^h = \bar{l}^h(L) \quad (-\psi^h)$$

$$x_i^h = \bar{x}_i^h \quad (-\gamma_i^h) \quad i = 1, \ldots, N.$$

We assume that the demand for good$i$ $(i = 1, \ldots, B)$ and the supply of labour are inelastic, at least locally. This hypothesis is realistic as long as one is dealing with 'small' tax variations. Indeed if these became too large the consumption of l^h and/or the private goods could fall beneath the respective upper bounds $\bar{l}^h$, $\bar{x}_i^h$, $i = (1, \ldots, N)$, in such a way that the consumer could no longer consider himself rationed. Programme (2.46) yields the following demand functions

$$l^h = \bar{l}^h(L)$$

$$x^h = \bar{x}^h(y) \tag{2.47}$$

$$z^h = z^h(q, r^h, \bar{x}^h, \bar{l}^h),$$

where we note the presence of two spill-over terms in the demand for Z which is the only commodity in the agents' consumption bundle to stay unrationed.

The excess supply of labour is still characterised as in the Keynesian regime (see 2.32) whereas the excess demand for good i is formulated as

$$\frac{\partial u^h}{\partial \bar{x}_i} > \varphi^h q_{x_i}, \quad \forall h, i. \tag{2.48}$$

In terms of the indirect utility function $V^h(q, r^h, \bar{x}, \bar{l}^h)$ we have

$$\frac{\partial V^h}{\partial q} = -\varphi^h C^h, \qquad \frac{\partial V^h}{\partial r^h} = \varphi^h, \qquad \frac{\partial V^h}{\partial \bar{l}^h} = \psi^h, \qquad \frac{\partial V^h}{\partial \bar{x}_i^h} = \gamma_i^h \tag{2.49}$$

(see Appendix 1 for a demonstration of these relations).

The private firm faces no constraint except for the usual technological one, so that its behaviour is quite standard since it maximises its profits (2.3) subject to the production function (2.2). The following supply and demand functions of the firm can be derived from the resolution of this programme (see 2.10)

$$s = s(p). \tag{2.50}$$

Equilibrium on the markets is essentially characterised by the following relations

$$\begin{aligned} y(p) &= e + \sum_h \bar{x}^h \underset{\text{def}}{=} e + \bar{x} \\ l^p(p) + l^z(z) &= \sum_h \bar{l}^h \underset{\text{def}}{=} L. \end{aligned} \tag{2.51}$$

The accounts of the public sector are written as

$$\begin{aligned} S(q, r, \bar{x}, L) = {} & (q_x - p_x)'\bar{x} + (p_l - q_l)l^p(p) \\ & + q_z z(.) - q_l l^z(z) - a(L^* - L). \end{aligned} \tag{2.52}$$

At this stage it is noteworthy that the public sector's decisions will have no effect whatsoever on the private sector's behaviour. Indeed since the level of output produced by the latter only depends on production prices, which are fixed and escape government control, the amount of private production, employment and therefore profits cannot be affected by changes in the consumer price system. Consequently the impact on welfare, which could be induced by governmental action in the classical regime, should be less significant than those in the Walrasian or Keynesian cases.

2.4.2 *Second-best optima*

The second-best problem to be solved is

$$\underset{(q,L)}{\text{Max}}\; W(q,r,\bar{x}^h,L)=\sum_h \mu^h V^h(q,r^h,\bar{x}^h,\bar{l}^h)$$
$$\text{s.t.}\quad L-l^p(p)-l^z(z)=0 \quad (-\nu) \tag{2.53}$$
$$S(q,r,\bar{x},L)=0 \quad (\rho)$$

Using the same type of proof as in Sub-Sections 2.2.2 and 2.3.2 it is easy to establish that, for the economy to be at a second-best optimum, the decision maker must find q and $\rho>0$ such that

$$\frac{1}{\rho}\sum_h \mu^h\varphi^h\left[C^h+(q_l-a-q_R^h)\left(1-\frac{\partial l^z}{\partial z}\frac{\partial z}{\partial L}\right)^{-1}\left(\frac{\partial l^z}{\partial z}\frac{\partial z}{\partial q}\right)\right]$$
$$=\left[\frac{\partial S}{\partial q}+\frac{\partial S}{\partial L}\left(1-\frac{\partial l^z}{\partial z}\frac{\partial z}{\partial L}\right)^{-1}\left(\frac{\partial l^z}{\partial z}\frac{\partial z}{\partial L}\right)\right] \tag{2.54}$$

where

$$\frac{\partial S}{\partial q}=\sum_h C^h+\left(q_z-q_l\frac{\partial l^z}{\partial z}\right)\frac{\partial z}{\partial q}+a\frac{\partial l^z}{\partial z}\frac{\partial z}{\partial q}$$

$$\frac{\partial S}{\partial L}=\left(q_z-q_l\frac{\partial l^z}{\partial z}\right)\frac{\partial z}{\partial l}+a\frac{\partial l^z}{\partial z}\frac{\partial z}{\partial l}+(p_l-q_l).$$

The same kind of cost-benefits analysis as in the Keynesian and Walrasian contexts (see (2.18) and (2.38)) applies to (2.54) and we shall not therefore carry it out again here. The most noticeable aspect of (2.54) however is that, contrary to the Walrasian and Keynesian cases, the agents' welfare and the public sector's accounts cannot be affected by variations in profits since, as we have already seen, all the components of the latter are fixed in the short run. Another point to be stressed is that the employment multiplier only takes into account the term $\partial l^z/\partial z$, i.e. variations in the demand for labour in the public sector, since l^p is not affected by changes in the consumer price vector. The relatively smaller magnitude of the employment multiplier in the classical regime is a standard property of disequilibrium models (see, for instance, Malinvaud, 1977) and is probably one of the major aspects of this theory in terms of economic policy. It emphasises how crucial it is to identify the actual unemployment regime, as the same policy measure might have a very different impact on the economy depending on the prevailing regime. Extreme examples of this are (i) an increase in public spending which will increase final demand and Keynesian employment but will have no effect on classical unemployment and (ii) an increase in real wages which will also decrease Keynesian unemployment but will increase classical un-

Table 2.1. *Needs for information*

	C^h	$\frac{\partial x}{\partial q}$	$\frac{\partial z}{\partial q}$	θ^h	$\frac{\partial l^p}{\partial y}$	$\frac{\partial l^z}{\partial z}$	$\frac{\partial x}{\partial L}$	$\frac{\partial z}{\partial L}$	$\frac{\partial x}{\partial r}$	$\frac{\partial z}{\partial r}$	q_R^h	$\frac{\partial p}{\partial q}$
Walrasian	×	×	×	×	×	×			×	×		×
Keynesian	×	×	×	×	×	×	×	×	×	×	×	
Classical	×		×			×		×			×	

employment. The problem is getting even more complex if both unemployment regimes are prevailing at the same time in the economy. This cannot but stress the need for developing methods enabling the government to define welfare improving tax directions whatever the unemployment regime is: this is the object of Sections 2.5 and 2.6.

Table 2.1 may be useful as it summarises the information needed by the public sector to implement a second-best optimum as a function of the state of the economy.

This table illustrates the fact that, for this model, the Keynesian regime is the most demanding in terms of information since it requires a knowledge of nearly all the parameters relevant to the economy. The classical regime is the least demanding as the parameters appertaining to the private production sector do not appear in (2.54). However in this case, the public sector should, as in the Keynesian regime, somewhat get information about the agents' reservation wages, which are unobservable. Let us finally observe that, since modifications in the consumption of private goods cannot be induced in this model and *a fortiori* since the agents' utilities are independent of such modifications, there is no need to estimate reservation prices for these commodities.

2.4.3 *Tax reform problem*

The tax reform problem for this economy is totally symmetrical to those considered in the two previous sections. We shall therefore study it rather briefly.

Let

$$(\partial V_C^h) = \frac{\partial V^h}{\partial q} + \frac{\psi^h}{\varphi^h}\left(1 - \frac{\partial l^z}{\partial z}\frac{\partial z}{\partial l}\right)^{-1}\left(\frac{\partial l^z}{\partial z}\frac{\partial z}{\partial q}\right) \tag{2.55}$$

or equivalently

$$(\partial C_C^h) - \varphi^h\left[C^h \quad (q_l - a - q_R^h)\left(1 - \frac{\partial l^z}{\partial z}\frac{\partial z}{\partial l}\right)^{-1}\left(\frac{\partial l^z}{\partial z}\frac{\partial z}{\partial q}\right)\right] \tag{2.56}$$

with, again, $(\partial V_C^h) = -(\partial C_C^h)$ and

$$(\partial S_C) = \frac{\partial S}{\partial q} + \frac{\partial S}{\partial L}\left(1 - \frac{\partial l^z}{\partial z}\frac{\partial z}{\partial l}\right)^{-1}\left(\frac{\partial l^z}{\partial z}\frac{\partial z}{\partial q}\right). \tag{2.57}$$

Equations (2.55) and (2.57) describe the reaction of a typical consumer and of the public sector respectively to a change dq.

A CITR requires to find dq's such that, for given $\tilde{\lambda}^h$'s

$$\sum_h \tilde{\lambda}^h (\partial C_C^h)' dq \leqslant 0 \tag{2.58}$$

and

$$(\partial S_C)' dq = 0. \tag{2.59}$$

Such directions will always exist as long as the economy is not at a second-best optimum for the particular $\tilde{\lambda}^h$'s.

For the PITR we must again define a few sets

$$\Lambda_C = [\lambda_C \,|\, \lambda_C \sum_h \lambda^h (\partial C_C^h),\ \lambda^h \geqslant 0] \tag{2.60}$$

$$\mathring{\Lambda}_C^* = [dq \,|\, \lambda_C' dq < 0,\ \forall \lambda_C \in \Lambda_C] \tag{2.61}$$

$$S_C^\perp = [dq \,|\, (\partial S_C)' dq = 0]. \tag{2.62}$$

The interpretation of these sets is identical to that given in Sections 2.2 and 2.3 for the Walrasian and Keynesian cases respectively.

Again it can be shown that PITR directions exist if

$$(\partial S_C) \subseteq \mathbf{C}\,(\Lambda_C \cup -\Lambda_C) \tag{2.63}$$

2.5 The 'uncertainty' case

One may now wonder whether PITR directions exist if one cannot positively decide what kind of unemployment, classical or Keynesian, prevails on the labour market. Much time and effort are often spent on determining whether the observed unemployment in a given economy is caused by a slackness in either the demand or the supply of consumer goods. This kind of debate might sometimes become useless if PID's could be determined whatever the prevailing regime.

However one should not be overoptimistic, and realise that it will be practically impossible to find a tax direction which will leave the public sector's budget unaffected, no matter what regime prevails. Indeed this would require vectors (∂S_K) and (∂S_C), expressing the marginal benefit to the public sector after a movement dq takes place, to be the same under both regimes: this is a rather strong – if not unrealistic – hypothesis.

One should thus satisfy oneself in looking for conditions of existence of tax movements which increase each individual's utility and also the public sector's surplus, thus creating inefficiencies whatever the regime. We say that such moves characterise a PITR in a 'weak' sense.

For the reader's facility we recall the following notation

$$\Lambda_K=[\lambda_K|\lambda_K=\sum_h \lambda^h(\partial C_K^h),\ \lambda^h\geqslant 0]$$

$$\Lambda_C=[\lambda_C|\lambda_C=\sum_h \lambda^h(\partial C_C^h),\ \lambda^h\geqslant 0].$$

Λ_K and Λ_C are thus the convex cones generated by all the positive linear combinations of the variations in the consumers' utilities after a modification in the tax vector in a Keynesian and classical regime respectively.

The positive polar cone to Λ_K (resp. Λ_C) is denoted Λ_K^* (resp. Λ_C^*) and is the set of all the tax moves increasing the agents utilities in a Keynesian (resp. classical) regime. We also have (∂S_K) and (∂S_C) which are the public sector's budget reaction vectors to dq for the two regimes and we denoted $S_K^{\perp}$, $S_C^{\perp}$ the orthogonal hyper-planes to (∂S_K) and (∂S_C) respectively. We now introduce the positive polar cones to both those vectors

$$S_K^*=[dq\,|\,(\partial S_K)'dq\leqslant 0]$$

$$S_C^*=[dq\,|\,(\partial S_C)'dq\leqslant 0],$$

i.e. the set of tax directions which decrease the public sector's surplus in the Keynesian and classical regimes respectively.

Preliminary hypotheses

The economy should first satisfy two preliminary and rather 'obvious' conditions.

*H*1: If one defines $\tilde{S}_K=\complement\, S_K^*$ and $\tilde{S}_C=\complement\, S_C^*$ one should have

$$\tilde{S}_K\cap\tilde{S}_C\neq\phi$$

or equivalently $(\partial S_K)\neq -k(\partial S_C), \forall k>0$.

$\tilde{S}_K$ (resp. $\tilde{S}_C$) is also the negative polar cone to (∂S_K) (resp. (∂S_C)) and is thus the set of all dq's such that $(\partial S_K)'dq\leqslant 0$ (resp. $(\partial S_C)'dq\leqslant 0$). *H*1 guarantees that there exists at least one tax direction which improves the public sector deficit in one regime without damaging it in the other.

*H*2: One should have $\mathring{\Lambda}_K^*\cap\mathring{\Lambda}_C^*\neq\phi$, that is, there exist tax directions which improve the agents' utility whatever the prevailing regime is. It is difficult to say whether *H*2 is a strong hypothesis. The following proposition may help us in this respect.

Proposition 4

$\mathring{\Lambda}^*_K \cap \mathring{\Lambda}^*_C \neq \phi \Leftrightarrow \mathring{\Lambda}_C \cap (-\mathring{\Lambda}_K) = \phi$.

Proof (a)$\Rightarrow$: if $\mathring{\Lambda}^*_C \cap \mathring{\Lambda}^*_K \neq \phi$ then

$$\exists \lambda \in (\mathring{\Lambda}^*_C \cap \mathring{\Lambda}_K)$$

and

$$\text{(i) } \lambda \in \mathring{\Lambda}^*_C \Rightarrow \mathring{\Lambda}_C \subseteq \lambda^*$$

where λ^* is the positive polar cone to λ and is here a half space;

$$\text{(ii) } \lambda \in \mathring{\Lambda}^*_K \Rightarrow \mathring{\Lambda}_K \subseteq \lambda^*.$$

This implies $-\mathring{\Lambda}_K \subseteq \complement\, \lambda^*$ and $\complement\, \lambda^*$ is a half space which proves that $\mathring{\Lambda}_C \cap (-\mathring{\Lambda}_K) = \phi$ as each convex cone $\mathring{\Lambda}_C$, $\mathring{\Lambda}_K$ is included in complementary half spaces.

(b)$\Leftarrow$: if $(\mathring{\Lambda}_C \cap -\mathring{\Lambda}_K) \neq \phi$ then

$$\exists l\colon l \in (\mathring{\Lambda}_C \cap \mathring{\Lambda}_K)$$

and

$$(\mathring{\Lambda}_C \cap -\mathring{\Lambda}_K)^* \subseteq l^*,$$

where l^* is the positive polar cone to l and is a half space.

As $l \in -\mathring{\Lambda}_K$, we have $(-\mathring{\Lambda}_k)^* e l^*$ and $\mathring{\Lambda}^*_K \subseteq \complement\, l^*$ so that $\mathring{\Lambda}^*_K \subseteq l^* = \phi$. Moreover we have $l \in \mathring{\Lambda}_C$ and $\mathring{\Lambda}^*_C \subseteq l^*$. Finally we have $\mathring{\Lambda}^*_C \cap \mathring{\Lambda}^*_K = \phi$. This is equivalent to proving

$$\mathring{\Lambda}_C \cap -\mathring{\Lambda}_K = \phi \Rightarrow \mathring{\Lambda}^*_C \cap \mathring{\Lambda}^*_K \neq \phi.$$

Q.E.D.

Proposition 4 states that for *H*2 to be fulfilled, the cone of consumption characterising one regime should not intersect with the opposite of the cone characterising the other regime. Intuitively for this situation to occur, it suffices that the consumers should not be net demanders of a particular good in one regime and net suppliers of it in the other.

Condition of existence of 'weak' PITR

Let us build two more sets, L^* and Σ:

$$L^* = \Lambda^*_K \cap \Lambda^*_C \quad \text{and} \quad L^* \neq \phi \quad by\ H2$$

$$\Sigma = [\sigma \mid \sigma = \sigma_1(\partial S_K) + \sigma_2(\partial S_C); \sigma_1, \sigma_2 \geqslant 0].$$

L^* is hence the convex cone including all the *dq*'s which improve the households' utility whatever the prevailing regime is. By H2, L^* is not empty.

Σ is the convex cone generated by the two vectors (∂S_K) and (∂S_C). It is thus the set of all positive linear combinations of these two directions.

Let Σ^* denote the positive polar cone to Σ and $\tilde{\Sigma}$ the negative polar cone to Σ (i.e. the set of tax directions which 'improve' any positive linear combination of (∂S_K) and (∂S_C)).

Proposition 5
'Weak' PITR directions exist for the two regimes if and only if

$$\Sigma \cap \text{conv}(\Lambda_K \cup \Lambda_C) = \phi, \tag{2.64}$$

where $\text{conv}(\Lambda_K \cup \Lambda_C)$ is the convex hull of $(\Lambda_K \cup \Lambda_C)$.

Proof (a)$\Rightarrow$: the existence of weak PITR is equivalent to saying that $L^* \cap \tilde{\Sigma} \neq \phi$. Now it is a standard property that $L^* = \Lambda_K^* \cap \Lambda_C^* = [\text{conv}(\Lambda_K \cup \Lambda_C)]^*$, so that we may define $L = \text{conv}(\Lambda_K \cup \Lambda_C)$.

We want to prove that $L^* \cap \tilde{\Sigma} \neq \phi x \Sigma n L = \phi$. This is quite obvious; since $L^* \cap \tilde{\Sigma} \neq \phi$ we may take $\tilde{d}q \in L^* \cap \tilde{\Sigma}$ and

$$\forall \sigma \in \Sigma : \sigma' \tilde{d}q \geqslant 0 \qquad \text{since} \quad \tilde{d}q \in \tilde{\Sigma}$$

$$\forall l \in L : l' \tilde{d}q \leqslant 0 \qquad \text{since} \quad \tilde{d}q \in L^*.$$

This proves that $\Sigma \cap L = \phi$ since the products $\sigma' \tilde{d}q$ and $l' \tilde{d}q$ are of opposite signs for all $\sigma \in \Sigma$ and $l \in L$.

(b)$\Leftarrow$: using the same kind of argument as in (a), one proves that $\Sigma \cap L - \phi \rightarrow L^* \cap \tilde{\Sigma} \neq \phi$.

Q.E.D.

The situations $\Sigma \cap L = \phi$ and $\Sigma \cap L \neq \phi$ are depicted on Figures 2.4 and 2.5 respectively.

Let us first note that $\Sigma \cap L = \phi$ implies that the economy cannot be a second-best optimum whatever the prevailing regime. Indeed since no element of Σ (i.e., any positive linear combination of (∂S_K) and (∂S_C)) can be included in L (i.e., the convex hull of the union of Λ_K and Λ_C), one has in particular $(\partial S_K) \notin \Lambda_K$ and $(\partial S_C) \notin \Lambda_C$ and thus the economy cannot be at a second-best optimum (see (2.38) and (2.54)). This is surely a natural condition since if it does not hold, say for the classical regime (so that $(\partial S_C) \in \Lambda_C$), it will not be possible to find tax directions increasing the agents' utilities although PID's may exist for the Keynesian case.

It is surely difficult to say whether $\Sigma \cap L = \phi$ is a strong condition or not. It depends totally on the structure of the sets defining Σ and L. The chances of finding weak PITR directions decrease if the vector (∂S_K) is very different from (∂S_C) and/or if Λ_K differs significantly from Λ_C, since in each of these cases Σ and/or L will get 'bigger' and thus the probability of having $\Sigma \cap L \neq \phi$ will grow. Now the main difference between the elements of Λ_K and Λ_C – out of which L is built – consists of the presence of profits and private employment multipliers in the former. If these are of greater magnitude than the common elements of Λ_K and Λ_C, i.e. essentially the agents' consumption bundles C^h's (see(2.40), (2.42), (2.56) and (2.60)), then the measure of L could be much bigger than the measure of the marginal utilities cones Λ_K, Λ_C.

The measure of Σ, on the other hand, will essentially depend on the magnitude of the terms $\partial x/\partial q$, $\partial x/\partial l$ and $\partial x/\partial r^h$ which appear in the definition of (∂S_K) (see (2.38) and (2.41)) but not in that of (∂S_C) (see (2.50)

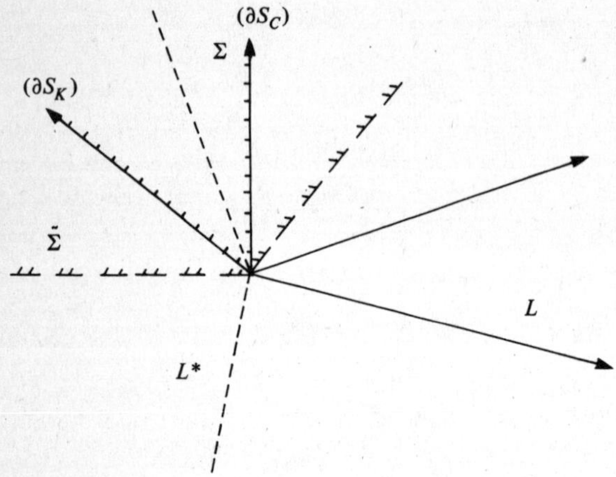

Figure 2.4 $\Sigma \cap L = \phi$

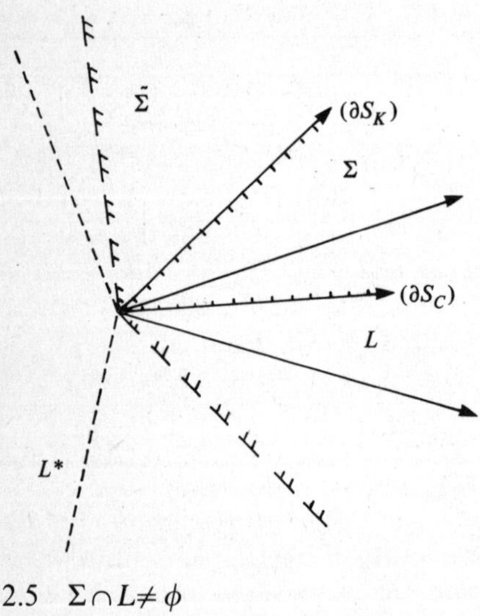

Figure 2.5 $\Sigma \cap L \neq \phi$

and (2.56)). The smaller these elasticities are – in absolute value – the smaller the measure of Σ will be since (∂S_K) and (∂S_C) will tend to coincide.

2.6 Mixed case

2.6.1 The agents

The last cases of second best and tax reform to be considered in this chapter deal with an economy in which the households suffer simultaneously from Keynesian and from classical unemployment. Needless to say, in such a situation we have to abandon the hypothesis of an aggregate private production sector and should instead split the latter into two sub-sectors – or firms. For notational convenience, we assume that each firm produces only one commodity. It is supposed that the first firm supplies good X_1 and operates in a Keynesian context, as expounded in Section 2.3, whereas the second firm produces commodity X_2 and operates as in Section 2.4, i.e. classically. The two firms, in order to produce their output, still need two inputs: labour and a commodity that is imported. The production price vector p has now four components, namely $p = (p_{x_1}, p_{x_2}, p_l, 1)$. We also denote π_1 (resp. π_2) the profits of the Keynesian (resp. classical) sector. Similarly $l_1(x_1)$ and $l_2(p)$ are the labour-demand functions of the two private firms.

Each household may now consume three goods (the two privately produced goods and commodity Z) but it faces two quantity constraints

$$
\begin{aligned}
&l^h = \bar{l}^h(L) \\
&x_2^h = \bar{x}_2^h(y_2)
\end{aligned}
\tag{2.65}
$$

where L is the total employment in the economy, y_2 is the aggregate production of commodity X_2 which only depends on p.

Household h still receives unemployment benefits and holds shares in both sub-sectors, hence $r^h = \theta_1^h \pi_1 + \theta_2^h \pi_2 + a(l^* - \bar{l}^h)$ and $\Sigma\theta_1^h = \Sigma\theta_2^h = 1$. Each agent maximises his utility under three constraints

$$
\begin{aligned}
&\text{Max } u^h(C^h) \\
&\text{s.t.} \quad q'C^h = r^h \\
&\qquad x_2^h = \bar{x}_2^h(y_2) \\
&\qquad l^h = \bar{l}^h(L).
\end{aligned}
\tag{2.66}
$$

The agents' demand functions derived from (2.66) are entirely symmetrical to those of Sections 2.3 and 2.4 (see (2.31) and (2.47)) and will thus not be reproduced here.

The amount of good Z produced by the public sector is still demand determined and requires only one input, i.e. labour. The public sector's accounts become

$$S=(q_x-p_x)'x+(p_l-q_l)(l_1+l_2)+q_z z-q_l l^z-a(L^*-L)$$

and (2.67)

$$L=l_1(x_1)+l_2(p)+l^z(z)$$

2.6.2 Second-best optima

In this case the decisions of the public sector are solution of the following problem

$$\max_{(q,r,L)} W(q,r,L)=\sum_h \mu^h V^h(q,r^h,\bar{x}_2^h,\bar{l}^h) \tag{2.68}$$

$$\begin{aligned} \text{s.t.}\quad & S(q,r,\bar{x}_2,L)=0 && (\rho)\\ & r^h-\theta_1^h\pi_1-\theta_2^h\pi_2-a(l^*-\bar{l}^h)=0 && (-\sigma^h),\quad \forall h\\ & L-l_1(x_1)-l_2(p)-l^z(z)=0 && (-\nu). \end{aligned}$$

Proposition 6

At the optimum of programme (2.68) the decision maker must find a vector q and a scalar $\rho>0$ such that $S=0$ and

$$\sum_h \mu^h\varphi^h\left[C^h-\theta_1^h\frac{d\pi_1}{dq}-(q_l-a-q_R^h)\frac{dL^K}{dq}\right] = \rho\left(\frac{\partial S}{\partial q}+\frac{\partial S}{\partial r}\frac{d\pi_1}{dq}+\frac{\partial S}{\partial L}\frac{dL^K}{dq}\right) \tag{2.69}$$

where

$$\frac{\partial S}{\partial q}=\sum_h C^h+(q_{x_1}-p_{x_1})\frac{\partial x_1}{\partial q}+(p_l-q_l)\frac{\partial l_1}{\partial x_1}\frac{\partial x_1}{\partial q} +\left(q_z-q_l\frac{\partial l^z}{\partial z}\right)\frac{\partial z}{\partial q}+a\left(\frac{\partial l_1}{\partial x_1}\frac{\partial x_1}{\partial q}+\frac{\partial l^z}{\partial z}\frac{\partial z}{\partial q}\right)$$

$$\begin{aligned}\frac{\partial S}{\partial r}&=\sum_h \theta_1^h\frac{\partial S}{\partial r^h}\\ &=\sum_h \theta_1^h\left[(q_{x_1}-p_{x_1})\frac{\partial x_1^h}{\partial r^h}+(p_l-q_l)\frac{\partial l_1}{\partial x_1}\frac{\partial x_1^h}{\partial r^h}\right.\\ &\qquad\left.+\left(q_z-q_l\frac{\partial l^z}{\partial z}\right)\frac{\partial z}{\partial r^h}+a\left(\frac{\partial l_1}{\partial x_1}\frac{\partial x_1^h}{\partial r^h}+\frac{\partial l^z}{\partial z}\frac{\partial z^h}{\partial r^h}\right)\right]\end{aligned}$$

$$\frac{\partial S}{\partial L} = (q_x - p_x)'x + (p_l - q_l)\left(1 + \frac{\partial l_1}{\partial x_1}\frac{\partial x_1}{\partial L}\right) + \left(q_z - q_l\frac{\partial l^z}{\partial z}\right)\frac{\partial z}{\partial L}$$

$$+ a\left(\frac{\partial l_1}{\partial x_1}\frac{\partial x_1}{\partial L} + \frac{\partial l^z}{\partial z}\frac{\partial z}{\partial L}\right)$$

$$\frac{\partial L^K}{\partial q} = \left(\frac{\partial l_1}{\partial x_1}\frac{\partial x_1}{\partial q} + \frac{\partial l^z}{\partial z}\frac{\partial z}{\partial q}\right)$$

$$\frac{\partial \pi_1}{\partial \tau} = \left(p_{x_1} - p_l\frac{\partial l_1}{\partial x}\right)\frac{\partial x_1}{\partial \tau} \qquad \text{for} \quad \tau = (q, r, L).$$

$$\begin{pmatrix} \dfrac{dL^K}{dq} \\[2mm] \dfrac{d\pi_1}{dq} \end{pmatrix} = \begin{pmatrix} \dfrac{\partial L^K}{\partial q} \\[2mm] \dfrac{\partial \pi_1}{\partial q} \end{pmatrix} \cdot \begin{pmatrix} 1 - \left(\dfrac{\partial l_1}{\partial x_1}\dfrac{\partial x_1}{\partial l} \quad \dfrac{\partial l^z}{\partial z}\dfrac{\partial z}{\partial l}\right) & -\dfrac{\partial \pi_1}{\partial l} \\[2mm] -\left(\dfrac{\partial l_1}{\partial x_1}\dfrac{\partial x_1}{\partial r} + \dfrac{\partial l^z}{\partial z}\dfrac{\partial z}{\partial r}\right) & 1 - \dfrac{\partial \pi_1}{\partial r} \end{pmatrix}^{-1}$$

The demonstration of Proposition 6 is similar to those of Sections 2.2 and 2.3 and will not be carried out here.

These results call however for a few remarks. First, and in view of (2.69), it appears that the decision maker must again strike a balance between the agents' utilities and the incidence of dq on the public sector's accounts.

Let us notice that the profits and employment multipliers intervening in (2.69) are not much more complex than those appearing in the first-order conditions of the 'pure' Keynesian and classical cases (see (2.38) and (2.54)). Indeed, since the profits and the employment of the classical firm cannot be affected by changes in the tax vector, the profit multiplier $d\pi_1/dq$ only concerns the impact of dq on the profits of the Keynesian firm. In the same way, the term dL^K/dq only concerns employment variations in the public and the Keynesian sector.

These changes in the definition of the profits and employment multipliers imply that the vector characterising the impact of dq on a given consumer's utility in the mixed case is not a mere convex combination of the corresponding expressions in the pure Keynesian and classical cases. The same remark naturally applies to the vector characterising the incidence of a tax move on the public sector's budget, i.e. the right-hand side of (2.69) cannot be written as a convex combination of the right-hand side of (2.38) and (2.54) (for a proof of this non-convexity, see Appendix 3).

In other words, and denoting (∂W_K) and (∂W_C) the marginal costs implied by dq at the optimum when the economy operates in a Keynesian regime and a classical regime respectively, we cannot conclude that, if the economy operates actually in a 'mixed' context, the impact of dq 'lies' somewhere in-between (∂W_K) and (∂W_C). This is most unfortunate since, as we shall see below, more information needs to be collected in the 'mixed' regime than in the 'pure' ones.

The second important point to be noticed is that the information needed by the decision maker in the mixed case is much more difficult to obtain than in the previous models. Besides estimating price- and income-derivatives, reservation wages and employment multipliers, the government must also be able to distinguish between the firms operating in a Keynesian context and those forming the classical sector. Likewise, it will have to determine in what measure each household may be affected by variations in the labour requirements of the Keynesian sector.

The first aspect of this information problem (i.e. which firms are in which regime) has already been successfully dealt with by J.-P. Lambert (1986) who, in an econometric disequilibrium model of Belgium, uses sample data concerning firms to estimate what share of the manufacturing sector is behaving Keynesianwise and what share classicalwise. The information concerning households would be much costlier to gather and to the best of our knowledge such information has never been collected to date.

2.6.3 Tax reform problem

The tax reform problem in this context is of course symmetrical to those studied in Sub-Sections 2.2.3, 2.3.3 and 2.4.3. We shall hence limit ourselves to state the main results for the economy under consideration.

Let us first define

$$(\partial C_M^h) = C^h - \theta_1^h \frac{d\pi_1}{dq} - (q_l - a - q_R^h)\frac{dL^K}{dq}, \quad h = 1, \ldots, H$$

$$(\partial S_M) = \frac{\partial S}{\partial q} + \frac{\partial S}{\partial r}\frac{d\pi_1}{dq} + \frac{\partial S}{\partial L}\frac{dL^K}{dq}. \tag{2.70}$$

(∂C_M^h) and (∂S_M) denote the impact of dq on household h's welfare and on the public finances respectively.

We also define Λ_M the cone generated by the (∂C_M^h)'s

$$\Lambda_M = [\lambda_M \mid \lambda_M = \sum_h \lambda^h(\partial C_M^h), \lambda^h \geqslant 0] \tag{2.71}$$

and its positive polar cone

$$\Lambda_M^* = [dq \mid \lambda_M' dq \leqslant 0, \forall \lambda_M \in \Lambda_M]. \tag{2.72}$$

Λ_M^* denotes the set of consumer price directions which decrease the cost of every agent's consumption.

It may be shown that PITR directions exist if and only if

$$(\partial S_M) \subseteq \mathbf{C}\,(\Lambda_M \cup -\Lambda_M). \tag{2.73}$$

As in the previous cases, 'weak' PITR directions (i.e. directions creating a surplus of the public sector's budget) exist if

$$(\partial S_M) \subseteq -\Lambda_M. \tag{2.74}$$

These results call for little comment except for one point: as has been noted before, for any h, the vector (∂C^h_M) is not necessarily equal to some convex combination of the vectors (∂C^h_K) and (∂C^h_C) (see (2.40), (2.56) and (2.69)). The same holds for (∂S_M) with respect to (∂S_K) and (∂S_C). This non-convexity implies that a tax direction which improves welfare in the mixed case need not be a convex combination of tax directions improving welfare in Keynesian and classical regimes. Moreover it also implies that a tax direction which is weakly Pareto improving in the uncertainty case (see Section 2.5) is not weakly Pareto improving in the mixed case, and conversely. Indeed since (∂C^h_M) $((\partial S_M))$ is not necessarily a convex combination of (∂C^h_K) $((\partial S_K))$ and of (∂C^h_C) $((\partial S_C))$, it cannot be concluded that Λ_M (i.e., the cone spanned by the (∂C^h_M)'s) is included in conv$(\Lambda_K \cup \Lambda_C)$ and that $(\partial C^h_M) \subseteq \Sigma$ (i.e., the cone spanned by (∂S_K) and (∂S_C)). Since the condition for having a weakly Pareto improving direction in the uncertainty case is $\Sigma \cap \text{conv}(\Lambda_K \cup \Lambda_C) = \phi$ (see (2.64)), it cannot be concluded that a tax direction improving welfare in this case will improve welfare in the mixed situation. As pointed out earlier, this means, that in order to increase welfare, the government cannot satisfy itself with collecting information as to how the economy would behave in a Keynesian and a classical regime and then deduce, out of this information, a welfare improving tax direction for the 'mixed' regime.

2.7 Conclusions

We had two main objectives in this chapter: the first one was to develop a theoretical framework stressing the link between PITR and second-best policies for different states – or regimes – of the economy. For each regime – Walrasian, Keynesian and classical – we also pointed out the set of information needed by the planner in order to implement a tax reform, or a second-best optimum. As may be seen from Table 2.1, these sets differ from one another essentially by their including or not profits and employment multipliers. The composition of these multipliers also changes from one regime to another.

The very fact that these multipliers emerge naturally from a general (dis)equilibrium framework is certainly noteworthy. As already stated in the Introduction, this property implies that, under suitable assumptions, second-best, tax reform, and cost-benefit analyses provide decision rules which reconcile micro- and macroeconomic thinking. General disequilibrium analysis is therefore the most appropriate approach to study public sector's policies since it enables the decision maker to take account of the aggregate impact on the economy without 'omitting' redistributive considerations.

The second objective was to derive easily estimable results for a 'realistic' economy. Our formulae (see (2.18), (2.38) and (2.54) are readily interpretable and, if one excepts the reservation wage appearing in (2.38) and (2.54), do not contain non-estimable parameters. Some difficulties may arise though when one tries to collect data concerning the individual agents' behaviour since these may sometimes be unreliable or confidential (as is the case in Belgium). But we shall turn our attention to that point in Chapter 5.

Several extensions of the model presented here may be considered but we have discarded them on the grounds of economic unrealism (lump-sum transfer policies, for instance) or because they do not affect the main characteristics of the obtained results (we especially think here of profit taxation and of the automatic indexation scheme of wages which is typical to Belgium).

3 Determination of Pareto improving directions

In the first section of this chapter we present a procedure that can be used to check whether a PITR exists and if so, also determines the 'best' tax direction associated to a given social welfare function. If the economy is already at a second-best optimum, we propose an easy way to track down the associated social weights. However if these do not match the public sector's views on redistribution, the latter may wish to depart from the existing situation even if by doing so it decreases some agents' utility. Two algorithms which may be helpful to determine CITR movements are analysed in Section 2.

In the remainder of this chapter we assume that the economy evolves in a Walrasian context. The results for the other regimes are simply obtained by adapting the notation when required.

3.1 PITR directions

Checking whether $(\partial S) \in \mathbf{C}\, \Lambda \cup -\Lambda$ holds, i.e. whether there exists a tax change dq such that $(\partial S)'dq = 0$ and $(\partial C^h)'dq \leqslant 0$, $\forall h$, can be accomplished by maximising a linear function of the agents' utilities subject to no one being made worse off and to a constraint on the public sector's budget. More formally, the following programme is to be solved

$$\operatorname*{Max}_{dq} - \sum_h \lambda^h (\partial C^h)'dq \tag{3.1}$$

$$\text{s.t.} \quad (\partial C^h)'dq \leqslant 0, \quad \forall h$$

$$(\partial S)'dq = 0$$

$$\sum_i^N |dq_i| \leqslant 1$$

where the λ^h's are arbitrarily fixed and positive.

The last constraint of this programme is a normalisation rule on dq which prevents us from dealing with an unbounded problem. Indeed, unless we impose such a constraint and since we are interested in small directions, any solution to (3.1) will only be defined up to a positive multiplicative constant implying also that welfare could be increased as much as we please.

Formulation (3.1) also makes very clear that the probability of finding PID's decreases as the number of households defining extreme directions of the cone Λ (i.e. constraints which are not positive linear combination of some others) increases with respect to the number of instruments at hand.

If problem (3.1) does not accept a feasible solution then, as we have seen in the previous chapter (cf. Proposition 2), there exists at least one set of coefficients λ^h's such that $(\partial S) = \sum_h \lambda^h (\partial C^h)$ with the λ^h's being all positive or all negative at the same time (i.e. $(\partial S) \in \Lambda$ and $(\partial S) \in -\Lambda$ respectively).

In that case checking whether $(\partial S) \in -\Lambda$ can also be done by solving a fairly simple linear programme. Indeed it suffices to look for a direction dq which does not make anyone worse off but which, at the same time, increases the public sector revenue. The following programme yields such a direction, provided it exists

$$\operatorname*{Max}_{dq} \ (\partial S)' dq \tag{3.2}$$

$$\text{s.t.} \quad (\partial C^h)' dq \leqslant 0, \quad \forall h$$

$$\sum_{i}^{N} |dq_i| \leqslant 1.$$

A non-zero solution to programme (3.2) indicates that PID's can be implemented but at the cost of inefficiencies. On the other hand, an optimal solution equal to zero combined with the unfeasibility of programme (3.1) implies that the economy is already at a second-best optimum for a certain distribution of the welfare weights. Actually, and in the general case $H > N$, it is expected that there exist many sets of positive coefficients λ^h's respecting (2.18). In fact, if (∂S) is in the interior of Λ, it could be written as a positive linear function of some of the combinations of $N+i$ $(i = 0, \ldots, H-N)$ vectors (∂C^h) taken in H. The total number of combinations to be examined is $L = \sum_{i=0}^{H-N} \binom{N+i}{H}$. If the public sector wants to know all the sets of weights underlying social welfare functions for which the economy is already at a second-best optimum, it will hence have to solve L systems of N equations of the type $(\partial S) = \sum_h \lambda^h (\partial C^h)$ with the number of unknowns, i.e. the λ^h's, varying between N and H. For each of the L combinations we may define a vector e_i $(i = 1, \ldots, L)$ such that $e_i \in \mathbb{R}^H$ and

$$e_{ih} = 1 \quad \text{if} \quad (\partial C^h) \text{ is included in the } i\text{th combination}$$

$$e_{ij} = 0 \quad \text{otherwise.}$$

To determine whether there exists a set of weights λ^h's such that the economy is at a second-best optimum for the ith combination of the vectors (∂C^h), it is necessary to solve a system of inequalities (namely, find $\lambda^h \geqslant 0$ for all h such that (∂C^h) is included in the ith combination) together with the second-best optimum condition, $\sum \lambda^h(\partial C^h) = (\partial S)$. This system of inequalities can be solved by maximising any function of the unknown λ^h's subject to the above-mentioned constraints. If we choose to maximise the sum of the λ^h's, the programme to solve is

$$\max_{\lambda^h} \sum_h \lambda^h \tag{3.3}$$

$$\text{s.t.} \quad \sum_h \lambda^h(\partial C^h) = (\partial S)$$

$$\lambda^h \geqslant 0 \quad \text{if} \quad e_{ih} = 1, \quad i = 1, \ldots, L$$

$$\lambda^h = 0 \quad \text{if} \quad e_{ih} = 0$$

$$\sum_h \lambda^h \leqslant 1.$$

Each feasible solution to these L programmes yields a set of coefficients for which the corresponding social welfare function is maximised by the existing tax vector.

At this stage the government may consider that none of the various sets reflects its views on social justice and may hence wish to implement a tax direction increasing the value of a social welfare function better fitted to its distribution aims. Two procedures which may help it in this respect are proposed in the next section.

3.2 CITR directions

3.2.1 Gradient projection algorithm (GPA)

This procedure is not new in the economic literature (see, for instance, d'Aspremont and Tulkens, 1980) and more specifically in the field of tax reform (see Guesnerie and Tirole, 1981).

Let us first examine how this algorithm works in the general case. Given $W(x)$ an objective function to be maximised subject to several constraints $[G_1(x), \ldots, G_M(x)]$, the GPA consists in projecting the gradient of $W(x)$ (noted ∇W) onto a linear approximation of the feasible set defined by the constraints. Let ∇G be the matrix formed by $(\nabla G_1, \ldots, \nabla G_M)$. Then the projection operator on the orthogonal complement of the space spanned by the columns of ∇G writes down as

$$P(x) = I - \nabla G(\nabla G' \nabla G)^{-1} \nabla G'. \tag{3.4}$$

The gradient projection of the objective function is

$$\nabla W_P = P(x) \nabla W. \tag{3.5}$$

Defining $\alpha(x) = (\nabla G' \nabla G)^{-1} \nabla G' \nabla W$, (3.5) can be alternatively formulated as

$$\nabla W_P = \nabla W - \nabla G \alpha(x). \tag{3.6}$$

The latter is especially convenient and intuitively appealing if the number of constraints is small, such as in our tax reform problem where we seek tax changes dq increasing a given social welfare function subject to a unique constraint on the public sector's budget. Applying (3.6) to this problem yields

$$dq = \sum_h \lambda^h (\partial V^h) - \alpha(dq)(\partial S) \tag{3.7}$$

where $\alpha(dq) = \dfrac{(\partial S)'[\Sigma \lambda^h (\partial V^h)]}{\|\partial S\|^2}$

and $\|\,.\,\|^2$ denotes the square of the Euclidean norm of a vector.

If $\alpha(dq)$ is negative then the interpretation of (3.7) could be the following:

(i) in a first step the price of a good is reduced proportionally to a weighted sum of the agents' marginal utilities with respect to this good;

(ii) in a second step the same price is increased (since $\alpha(dq) < 0$) in proportion to the budget surplus generated by a unit increase in the very same price.

$\alpha(dq)$ positive would imply that an increase in the tax rates has a negative impact on the public sector's budget. Indeed since the different components of the vector defined by $\sum_h \lambda^h (\partial V^h)$ are negative (except for the term relative to wage) and in view of $\alpha(dq) > 0$, one should have $(\partial S)' dq < 0$. In this case, the second step of the procedure would be undesirable.

3.2.2 The Ahmad–Stern approach

Ahmad and Stern (1984) propose another method for finding CITR directions. They are not looking for an optimal path – in the way the GPA does – but they are trying to determine which goods could be more heavily taxed and which could be taxed less in such a way that the agents' utility would be increased without perturbing the public sector's balance. This approach is not really a maximisation procedure and should be in this respect less 'optimal' than the GPA but may be politically more easily applicable.

The authors' argument is fairly simple. If one denotes $\partial S/\partial q_i$ the ith component of vector (∂S), the change in q_i required to yield an extra franc of revenue to the government is given by $(\partial S/\partial q_i)^{-1}$. The fall in social welfare resulting from such a change is

$$\mu_i = -\frac{\partial W}{\partial q_i}\left(\frac{\partial S}{\partial q_i}\right)^{-1} \tag{3.8}$$

where $\dfrac{\partial W}{\partial q_i}$ denotes the ith component of the vector formed by $\sum_h \lambda^h(\partial V^h)$.

If $\mu_i > \mu_j$ one can improve the social welfare by increasing q_j just enough to raise one franc and by reducing equivalently q_i, since the situation $\mu_i > \mu_j$ means that the social loss incurred from the increase of q_j is more than offset by the welfare obtained through the reduction in q_i.

3.3 Concluding remarks

The algorithms proposed above are intuitively appealing and also quite easily applicable. They either make use of standard linear programming techniques (Section 3.1) or can be applied directly once the computation of the vectors (∂S) and (∂W) have been carried out (Section 3.2).

A more general remark as to the size of the reform is however in order. Tax reform finds its *raison d'être* in the observation that small tax movements are politically more acceptable than large ones. Since these political constraints can hardly be modelled in a general framework, it is up to the decision maker to decide in each situation upon the magnitude of the reform.

A more technical aspect should also be taken into consideration. Tax reform relies indeed on the computation of local properties of the economy (e.g., price- and income-elasticities). If one believes that these properties remain valid even for large variations of the tax rates, then one may consider a 'non-marginal' tax reform.

Our strategy in the next chapter is the following: first we compute the vectors (∂S) and (∂C^h)'s, then we test by applying procedure (3.1), and possibly (3.2), whether directions of tax reform existed in Belgium in 1982. If the space of PID's appears to be empty, we then endeavour to determine, by applying (3.3), the weights associated to the social welfare functions with respect to which the economy was already at a second-best equilibrium. We eventually carry out simulations using the results of Section 3.2 in order to compute tax directions increasing the welfare for alternative values of these social weights.

4 An economic model of Belgium

4.1 Introduction

In this chapter we estimate all the relations needed to compute a vector (∂S) for Belgium in 1982, namely a matrix of price and income elasticities for several consumer goods and the multipliers effects of profits $\left(\frac{d\pi}{dq}\right)$ and employment $\left(\frac{dL}{dq}\right)$. The actual computation of vector (∂S) will take place in the next chapter. Our first task however is to determine which unemployment regime prevailed in Belgium in 1982. The sample survey carried out by the Banque Nationale among the firms helps us in this respect, as part of it consists in determining whether firms are constrained and, if so, what kind of constraint they perceive. In June 1982 (see Banque Nationale de Belgique, 1982), 82 percent of firms questioned admitted being constrained by demand. In each sector of the economy – the synthetic fibres and motorcycle manufacturing sectors – the majority of the firms perceived this type of constraint. At the same time, more than 12 percent of the total labour force was unemployed. We may therefore assume that globally, Belgium was then experiencing Keynesian unemployment which implies that we have to estimate the different components of formula (2.40) and (2.41) of Section 2.3.

One may object that a more appropriate approach would have been to take explicit account of the behaviour of the firms which were not in Keynesian regime. However, in view of the fairly small percentage of 'classical' firms and in order to facilitate the econometric modelling, we feel inclined to assume that in 1982 the Belgian economy was, on the whole, operating in a Keynesian context. Nevertheless, we shall come back to this point later on in this chapter.

Let us first examine – very briefly – the economic situation in Belgium in 1982. As can be seen in Table 4.1, the economy was essentially characterised by huge disequilibria: unemployment and the public sector

Table 4.1. *Main indicators*

	1978	1979	1980	1981	1982
GNP (current prices × 10^9 BF)	3,061.8	3,254.3	3,482.6	3,621.4	3,902.8
GNP (1975 prices)	2,549.2	2,601.6	2,670.0	2,637.9	2,657.0
Constituents of GNP					
Private consumption (in %)	61.7	63.0	64.1	66.1	66.6
Public consumption	17.8	18.1	18.5	19.4	19.0
Investment	21.4	21.0	20.9	17.7	16.8
Net exports	−0.8	−2.1	−3.5	−3.1	−2.4
Unemployment (as % of active population)	7.3	7.7	8.1	10.4	12.2
Public deficit as % of GDP	7.1	7.6	10.9	14.4	14.1
Consumer price index	3.9	3.7	7.0	8.7	7.5
Income structure (as % of national income)					
Wages	70.9	72.7	73.8	74.6	73.5
Proprietors' income	15.4	14.7	13.8	13.6	13.9
Capital income	13.5	14.2	15.2	17.0	18.0
Retained earnings	0.9	0.9	0.7	0.4	0.9
Interests on public debt	−5.5	−6.2	−7.5	−9.8	−11.5
Others	4.8	3.7	4.0	4.2	5.2

Source: I.N.S.

deficit were at their highest while the trade balance deficit finally began to fall thanks to the combined actions of an 8.5 percent devaluation of the Belgian Franc and a slowdown in domestic demand. Finally, and as if even more gloom was needed in this already depressing picture, private investment collapsed and fell by more than 20 percent in less than four years.

The private production sector, however, began to show signs of brighter days (see Table 4.2). Profits increased very sharply from 1981 to 1982 and the number of firms suffering losses, although still high, was at its lowest level for five years. This evolution may be explained by the improved competitiveness of Belgian firms on foreign markets (due to the devaluation and to the curb on wages imposed by the government) and also because a lot of less profitable firms had been swept out of the economy in the previous years of the crisis. Prospects, however, still looked bleak and did not induce firms to take on more workers.

As can be seen in Table 4.3 and Figure 4.1, the situation in the public sector could be described as going from bad to worse. Although the Social Security deficit continued to represent a substantial but constant share of GDP, the overall public sector deficit more or less doubled between 1979 and 1981. Several reasons may be put forward to explain this dramatic increase: the huge amount of interest on the public debt, the cost of

Table 4.2. *Firms' situation*

	1978	1979	1980	1981	1982
Number of bankruptcies[1]	2,692	2,918	3,538	4,150	4,251
Percentage of firms suffering losses[2]	29.6	27.3	29.3	31.0	26.3
Gross profits ($\times 10^9$ BF)[3]	252.2	313.0	297.2	307.3	397.9
Net results[4]	19.0	45.8	−1.2	−21.8	54.3

[1] *Source:* I.N.S.
[2] *Source:* Banque Nationale.
[3] *Source:* Banque Nationale. Concerns non-financial firms. Gross profits equal value added minus wages.
[4] Gross profits minus transfers to reserves exempted from taxation.

Table 4.3. *State's situation*

	1978	1979	1980	1981	1982
Public deficit ($\times 10^9$ BF)	233.8	284.8	372.4	526.8	605.7
Social security deficit ($\times 10^9$ BF)	197.9	210.1	225.7	291.0	333.4
State's financial income ($\times 10^9$ BF)	850.3	905.9	946.2	953.4	1076.1
Personal income tax	293.477	326.761	364.697	394.042	430.694
V.A.T.	236.969	237.222	253.497	258.075	276.974
Excise and other consumption taxes	71.680	75.593	77.244	70.267	79.872
Corporate tax	7.001	3.006	2.644	−1.248	7.725

Source: I.N.S.

programmes designed to decrease unemployment (early retirement schemes, creation of jobs of collective interest, ...) and the loss of fiscal income due to flagging activity. In this latter respect, it is significant that the share of labour income tax which amounted to 36 percent of total state income in 1979 climbed to 40 percent in 1982, while the share of total consumption taxes dropped during the same period from 34.5 percent to 33 percent.

Several studies have tried to show the main causes of this sharp and long-lasting slump. Nearly all of them reach the same conclusions as to what concerns unemployment. Firstly, during the seventies, there was an increase in real wages in Belgium which exceeded that of most of its international competitors (see Drèze and Sneessens, 1986). These excessive real wages have been somewhat exacerbated by the tendency of successive governments to increase taxes on labour and subsidise capital investment.

This somewhat short-sighted policy, combined with other factors explaining wage rigidity (e.g., automatic wage indexation and minimum wages) has encouraged firms to maintain or shift their production to less labour intensive activities. Secondly, effective demand has slowed down since the first oil crisis onwards. At this level, structural considerations should also enter the picture. As noted by the OECD (1984) and the Banque Nationale de Belgique (1980) the Belgian production apparatus seems to be ill-adapted to world demand. The implication of this mismatch between Belgian supply and foreign demand is better understood when one remembers that Belgian exports represent more than 60 percent of GNP. Thirdly, the unemployment level rose due to the emergence of women on the labour market. This increase in the active population could not all be absorbed by an already ailing economy.

Quite clearly, fiscal policy cannot, on its own, take up the challenges represented by ageing industries or by sociological changes. The sole aim of this work is to check whether, given the context described above, the public sector is left with any margin of manoeuvre in its attempt to increase individual utilities through fiscal policies without increasing its deficit any further. If such a margin exists, the changes advocated should intuitively stimulate demand and possibly employment. It is also obvious, however, that the public sector will never – at least not in the foreseeable future!

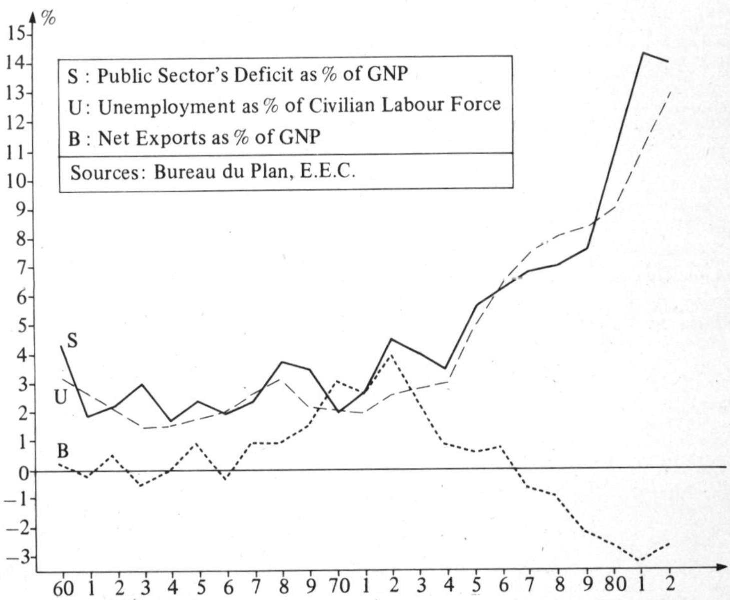

Figure 4.1 Unemployment, trade and public deficit

– be in possession of all the information necessary to build a vector (∂C^h_K) for every household in the economy and, even if it did, the probability of finding Pareto improvements for all of them would normally tend to zero (see Chapter 3).

Therefore, the attitude adopted here consists in selecting a few households, each of which is representative of a whole class of agents. However convenient, this strategy will lead, as we shall see in the following pages, to some difficulties in interpreting the final results.

We may now examine, step by step, what are the various econometric estimations needed to compute vector (∂S_K). This is how the model proceeds (see also Figure 4.2):

1 When a tax variation takes place, consumers adapt their demand for the various goods. These variations in consumption can be estimated through a demand system for goods which takes into account the rationing scheme on the labour market. The estimation of such a demand system is taken up in Section 4.2. The vector $\frac{\partial S}{\partial q}$ appearing in (2.4) may be built at this stage since it consists of the 'direct' fiscal effects of a movement dq. We have however to depart from the theoretical model in one respect: wages and social benefits in Belgium are linked to consumer prices. This indexation scheme has not been considered in the theoretical

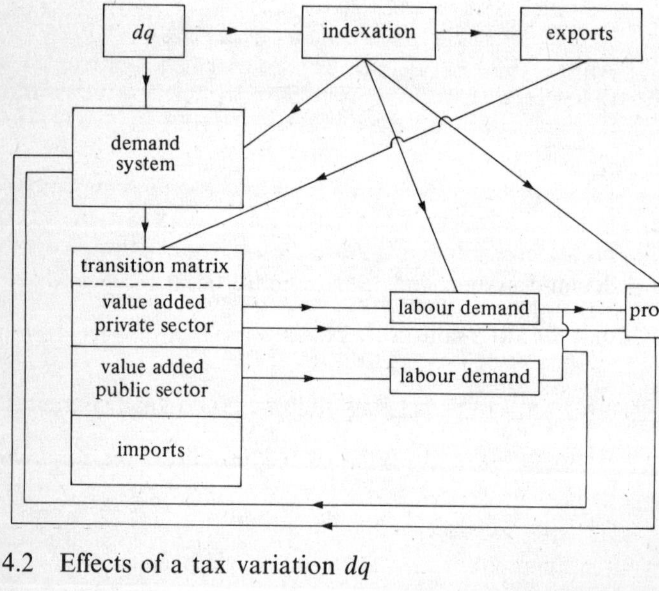

Figure 4.2 Effects of a tax variation dq

model essentially for reasons of notational clarity. It is clear that its introduction does not change the main spirit of the results of Chapter 2. To simplify the econometric modelling, we assume that wages are fully and immediately indexed.[1] However, the model takes into consideration the fact that the variation in income induced by the indexation process is taxed at what can be estimated to be the mean marginal rate of taxation, i.e., 45 percent (see Ministère des Finances, 1984).

2 The variations in consumers' demand have effects on production and imports. These effects are computed by means of a transition matrix based on the 1975 input–output matrix. It should be noted that the indexation scheme, which is borne by the employers, changes the production costs of commodities. These modifications in turn affect the level of Belgian exports and hence that of national production. The impact of wage indexation on exports is examined in Section 4.3, whilst the transition matrix is built in Section 4.4.

3 The variation in national production induced by the changes in private consumption and exports affects the demand for labour. Section 4.5 is devoted to the study of these effects in both the private and public production sectors. The induced changes in employment and production, combined with the indexation process, results in modifications of the private sector's profits. The latter are simply estimated as being equal to the variations in value added minus the variations in the wage bill. It is assumed for simplicity's sake that any variation in net profits is entirely redistributed among the shareholders. After paying a tax of 20 percent on dividends ('précompte mobilier'), shareholders should normally declare to the fiscal authorities their net gains which become part of their taxable income. In view of the high level of tax evasion in the Belgian economy, it is assumed, however, that this latter declaration is not effective. The observed variations in profits and employment are then introduced into the consumers' demand system and lead to more fiscal repercussions. We feel that the latter constitute good approximations to the terms $\frac{\partial S}{\partial r}\frac{d\pi}{dq}$ and $\frac{\partial S}{\partial L}\frac{dL}{dq}$ of (2.41). Although we could have continued with the computation and estimated further effects on employment and profits, we reckoned that, as fixed-price theory is only relevant

[1] Actually, in 1982, wages were indexed by an amount corresponding to the full indexation of the minimum wage.

in a short-run context, it was wiser to limit ourselves to these 'one-round' estimations of $\frac{d\pi}{dq}$ and $\frac{dL}{dq}$. Moreover, and as the following computations will show, these multipliers are of limited magnitude and thus considering higher order effects would only result in negligible changes in the final results.

At this stage, we are in possession of all the elements necessary to compute the global effect of a general tax increase on public sector finances (i.e., formula (2.41)): this estimation is carried out in the next chapter together with that of the consumption cone Λ_K and the computation of PITR directions.

4.2 System of demand equations

4.2.1 Introduction

Several models of systems of demand equations under quantity rationing have flourished in the literature during the last few years. All of these are natural extensions of 'unrationed' models: the 'Linear Expenditure System' (Ashenfelter, 1980), the 'Rotterdam System' (Bronsard and Bronsard, 1980) and the 'Almost Ideal System' (Deaton, 1981). Of all the models we tried, the Rotterdam System turned out to provide us with the most satisfying results. The goal of the present sub-section is to examine the theoretical properties of the model.

Recalling the results of Section 2.3, the demand functions of a typical consumer rationed on the labour market may be written as

$$x_j = x_j(\tilde{q}, I, l), \quad j = 1, \ldots, N \tag{4.1}$$

where $\tilde{q}$ is the $(N \times 1)$ vector of consumption prices,
I is the agent's total income and is equal to $\sum_j \tilde{q}_j x_j$.

In vector notation, one has

$$x = x(\tilde{q}, I, l). \tag{4.1'}$$

For notational convenience, we do not distinguish anymore between commodities produced by the private and by the public sector. Consequently, one or several components of vector x may represent goods produced by public enterprises.

Taking the differential of (4.1′) yields

$$dx = S d\tilde{q} + T' \tilde{q} dx + u dl \tag{4.2}$$

with

$$S: (N \times N), \qquad S = S', \qquad S\tilde{q} = 0 \quad \text{and} \quad S \text{ is s.d.n.}$$

$$T: (N \times 1), \qquad \tilde{q}'T = 1$$

$$u: (N \times 1), \qquad \tilde{q}'u = 0$$

(for a proof of these properties, see Bronsard and Bronsard, 1980).

Matrix S can be assimilated to the 'classical' Slutsky Matrix and T to the vector of income effects. We adopt the following notation:

$\imath$ is a $(N \times 1)$ vector of 1's,

for any vector v, diag(v) is a diagonal-matrix such that diag$(v)\cdot\imath = v$,

$\text{diag}(w) = (\text{diag}(q)\cdot\text{diag}(x))/I$.

(4.2) may now be written as

$$\text{diag}(w)\cdot\text{diag}(x)^{-1}dx = K\ \text{diag}(\tilde{q})^{-1}d\tilde{q} + \beta\frac{dI}{I} + v\frac{dl}{l} \tag{4.3}$$

subject to

$$K = K'$$

$$K'\imath = 0$$

$$v'\imath = 0$$

$$\beta'\imath = 1.$$

Finally (4.3) may be transformed into

$$\text{diag}(w)d\log \text{x} = Kd\log\tilde{q} + \beta d\log I + vd\log I + \varepsilon, \tag{4.4}$$

where ε is a vector of random variables with zero expectation and covariance matrix Ω.

4.2.2 Estimation

Model (4.4) has been estimated for the 7 following goods:

1 food, beverage and tobacco,
2 durables (including purchases of transportation material),
3 energy (including gasoline),
4 housing,
5 services and leisure,
6 communication and transport services,
7 clothing.

Table 4.4. *Compensated demand equations*[1]

	Income	Food	Durables	Energy	Housing	Services	Communic.	Clothing	Labour	R^2	$D-W$
Food	0.2114	−0.0606	0.0194	0.0081	0.0018	0.0007	0.0051	0.0254	0.0351	0.80	1.71
	(0.021)	(0.0024)	(0.014)	(0.009)	(0.011)	(0.021)	(0.004)	(0.008)	(0.031)		
Durables	0.3044		−0.0314	0.0108	−0.0238	0.0232	−0.0075	0.0093	0.0090	0.88	2.05
	(0.023)		(0.018)	(0.008)	(0.009)	(0.019)	(0.005)	(0.007)	(0.034)		
Energy	0.0961			−0.0297	0.0070	−0.0143	0.0034	0.0147	−0.0346	0.61	2.02
	(0.018)			(0.011)	(0.005)	(0.010)	(0.002)	(0.005)	(0.028)		
Housing	0.0741				0.0064	0.0126	−0.0055	0.0015	−0.0140	0.83	1.13
	(0.009)				(0.010)	(0.013)	(0.003)	(0.005)	(0.012)		
Services	0.2047					−0.0323	0.0052	0.0049	−0.0618	0.86	0.18
	(0.019)					(0.031)	(0.005)	(0.019)	(0.027)		
Communications	0.0080						0.0026	0.0018	0.0034	0.37	0.24
	(0.003)						(0.001)	(0.002)	(0.005)		
Clothing	0.1013							−0.0576	0.0628	0.88	1.94
	(0.009)							(0.006)	(0.013)		

[1] The R^2 statistics appearing in this table are adjusted for the absence of constant terms.

Consumption of commodities sold by the public sector is essentially represented by the sixth item. Data on consumption of annual aggregate time series are extracted from the National Accounts of Belgium (see I.N.S., 1983) and are divided by active population. The number of hours effectively worked per officially registered worker in the manufacturing sector is used as a proxy for the constraint on the labour market (see Appendix 4). These equations were estimated using the method advocated by Barten (1969) and over the period 1953–82. The results are to be found in Table 4.4.

The results are satisfactory, even if one may regret the wrong sign of the elasticity of 'housing' with respect to its own price. The fit of the equations relative to energy and communication services is unfortunately rather low. However, let us notice that these two items represent small shares of total expenditure. It appears that each marginal propensity to consume is positive and significative with 'durables' having the highest propensity (0.304) and 'communications' the lowest (0.008).

The rationing scheme on the labour market has a significant effect – at the 95 percent level – on services and clothing. Generally, the effect on consumption of an increase in this constraint has the expected sign.

Table 4.5 gives the results for the uncompensated demand equations. These call for little comment except that they will be used in the remainder of our study.

4.3 Exports

We now analyse the impact on exports of variations in the production costs generated by the indexation of wages. As is usual for models studying the trade equations of Belgium, it is assumed that Belgian producers are price takers on foreign markets. This hypothesis is typical of the concept of the 'small and open economy' and essentially implies that an increase in the production costs cannot be reflected in export prices. Instead, firms decrease their supply of goods on foreign markets.

The specification and estimation of the foreign trade equations have already been studied in many models (see Drèze and Modigliani, 1981). We adopt here the estimation carried out by the Bureau du Plan (1984) for the MARIBEL model, in which exports are written as a function of the volume of the international trade and of the firms' profit margin. This formulation expresses the assumption that the amount of Belgian exports is determined by world demand and that the share of the market fluctuates with export prices and production costs.

The estimation period covers the years 1962 to 1981 and concerns manufactured goods, less energy, which represent approximately 80 percent of total exports. Energy is excluded from this specification since

Table 4.5. *Uncompensated elasticities (1982)*

	β_i	Food	Durables	Energy	Housing	Services	Communic.	Clothing	v_i
Food	0.780	−0.430	−0.075	−0.040	−0.110	−0.150	0.004	0.028	0.130
Durables	1.610	−0.330	−0.470	−0.087	−0.370	−0.190	−0.071	−0.086	0.048
Energy	1.069	−0.198	−0.080	−0.430	−0.084	−0.368	0.017	0.074	−0.380
Housing	0.489	−0.120	−0.250	0.002	−0.030	−0.012	0.046	−0.031	−0.090
Services	1.045	−0.278	−0.079	−0.167	−0.094	−0.369	0.006	−0.063	−0.310
Communications	0.406	0.151	−0.458	0.137	−0.340	0.180	−0.139	0.058	0.170
Clothing	1.206	−0.024	−0.117	0.067	−0.165	−0.178	−0.002	−0.780	0.748

Table 4.6. *Elasticity of exports to wages in several models of the Belgian economy*

BREUGHEL	−0.22
DESMOS	−0.72
LINK	−0.60
RENA	−0.30
SERENA	−0.64

its production involves a specific cost structure which makes it rather inelastic to variations in the wage bill.[2] On the other hand, and once again according to the Bureau du Plan, the elasticity of services exports with respect to production costs is small and non-significative. This may be explained by the fact that services exports partly consist of items insensitive to price variations (such as commissions, patents, etc.).

These are the results obtained by the Bureau du Plan

$$\begin{aligned}\Delta \log E_t = {} & \underset{(7.7)}{0.959}[\underset{(37.4)}{1.123}\,\Delta \log WE_t + \underset{(1.76)}{0.584}\,\Delta \log(PE/CE)_t] \\ & + \underset{(3.8)}{0.951}[\underset{(411.2)}{6.74} + \underset{(37.4)}{1.12}\,\log WE_{t-1} + \underset{(1.76)}{0.584}\,\log(PE/CE)_{t-1}] \\ & - \underset{(3.8)}{0.951}\,\log E_{t-1} - \underset{(-2.1)}{0.049}\,tI_{(t<76)},\end{aligned} \tag{4.5}$$

where E_t is Belgian exports at time t,
WE_t is exports of industrial countries,
PE_t is price index of exports of goods (energy excluded),
CE_t is unit cost index of exports,
$I_{(t<76)}$ is an indicator function taking into account a change in the definition of the exports series which occurred in 1976.

(Values between brackets represent the t-ratios.)

The estimated short-run elasticity of exports with respect to production costs equals −0.58. The input–output table shows that wages represent a little more than a third of the costs necessary to produce a unit of a commodity to be exported. We may thus assume that −0.2 is an appropriate estimate of the short-run elasticity of exports to wages.

As may be seen in Table 4.6, this coefficient is smaller in absolute value than that obtained in models such as DESMOS, LINK or SERENA, but is of the same order of magnitude as in BREUGHEL and RENA.

[2] According to the 1975 input–output matrix, wages represented only 6.2 percent of the production cost of energy exports.

4.4 The transition matrix

4.4.1 Introduction

As we said before, we need to model activity at the industrial level before turning our attention to labour requirements. This implies that a link must be found between the various components of final demand and sectoral activity (i.e., production). Input–output theory can provide this link.

Let us first consider the general problem of converting final demand such as classified in the input–output matrix (i.e., private consumption, investment, exports and public expenditure) to output originating from the industrial sectors. The traditional input–output system can be solved for sales S in terms of final demand F

$$S = (I - A)^{-1}F, \tag{4.6}$$

where A is the matrix of technical coefficients indicating the amount of sector i's output needed to produce one unit of sector j's output $(i, j = 1, \ldots, M)$.

We now come up against two problems. The first is that, in the context of our model of tax reform, we need an aggregation on F different from that provided by the input–output matrix. Actually, we would like to disaggregate final demand into the seven private consumption items used in the demand system, exports and exogenous demand (i.e., investment and State's purchase). Secondly, for purposes of forecasting and simulating the impact of tax rate variations, we need long time series on sales. Such information is not available contrary to series concerning value added. Our task is thus to work out a relationship between the expenditure components of GNP and the value added by the industrial sectors.

Once the static input–output framework is accepted, there is then an obvious relationship between sales and value added since the difference between the two consists in the cost of intermediate goods. This relationship is expressed as

$$V = B \cdot S. \tag{4.7}$$

(4.7) relates sales to value added V through a matrix B whose typical element b_{ji} is such that

$$b_{ji} = 1 - \sum_{i=1}^{M} a_{ij}, \quad j = 1, \ldots, M$$

$$b_{ij} = 0, \quad i \neq j,$$

and the a_{ij}'s are the elements of A. Substituting (4.7) in (4.6) and solving for final demand yields

$$F = (I - A)B^{-1}V. \tag{4.8}$$

The elements of $(I - A)B^{-1}$, denoted w_{ij}, have the following property

$$\sum_{j}^{M} w_{ij} = 1, \quad i = 1, \ldots, M.$$

Equation (4.8) expresses final demand in terms of the value added by the industrial sectors. However, it is still necessary to adopt another disaggregation of final demand F which would better satisfy our requirements. This link may be provided by the industrial distribution of demand which is summarised by matrix D. This matrix has as many columns as there are expenditure categories (i.e., N) and as many lines as there are industrial sectors (i.e., M). A column of D provides the industrial distribution for a given expenditure category. One has

$$\sum_{j=1}^{M} d_{jk} = 1, \quad k = 1, \ldots, N.$$

Denoting E the final expenditure categories emanating from the GNP components, the following relationship holds

$$F = D \cdot E. \tag{4.9}$$

Substituting (4.9) into (4.8) and solving for value added yields

$$V = B(I - A)^{-1}DE \tag{4.10}$$

and matrix $B(I - A)^{-1}D$ is $(M \times N)$. If we define $C = B(I - A)^{-1}D$, (4.10) may be rewritten as

$$\begin{aligned} V_1 &= c_{11}E_1 + \cdots + c_{1N}E_N \\ &\vdots \\ V_M &= c_{M1}E_1 + \cdots + c_{MN}E_N \end{aligned} \tag{4.11}$$

and the following property is easily established

$$\sum_{j}^{M} c_{jk} = 1, \quad k = 1, \ldots, N,$$

so that

$$\sum_{j}^{M} V_j = \sum_{k}^{N} E_k = \text{GNP} \tag{4.12}$$

We have thus succeeded in formulating the required link between the value added by the production sector and the various categories of final demand.

There is still one problem to be solved however, if these results are to be used for forecasting in a period far removed from that of the construction of matrix G. The technical coefficients and the distribution

Table 4.7. *Transition matrix*

	Food	Durables	Energy	Housing	Services	Communications	Clothing	Exogeneous demand	Exports
Private sector	0.654	0.616	0.514	0.429	0.755	0.238	0.574	0.382	0.544
Public firms	0.005	0.008	0.003	0.006	0.014	0.594	0.005	0.008	0.010
Imports	0.341	0.436	0.484	0.097	0.229	0.168	0.430	0.277	0.450
Public administrations	0	0	0	0	0	0	0	0.330	0
Rents	0	0.010	0	0.466	0	0	0	0.002	0

of demand may vary widely through time. This could lead to serious error when converting final demand to value added and hence affects our predictions about profits and labour requirements.

One way of dealing with this problem is to express at each period t the observed values of imports and value added as a function of the result obtained by (4.11) and of a stochastic term, i.e.

$$V_{it} = f(C_i'E_{it}, u_t) \qquad \text{for} \quad i = 1, \ldots, M \qquad (4.13)$$
$$t = 1, \ldots, T.$$

In the next sub-section, we estimate matrix G and model more explicitly relation (4.13).

4.4.2 *Empirical results*

The input–output matrix we are working with dates from 1975 (see I.N.S., 1983) and carries information about fifty production sectors plus imports (see Appendix 5 for a list of these sectors). Matrix D is built by the I.N.S. and is given in Appendix 6. Using (4.10) we have computed the transition matrix G between the fifty-one items of the input–output matrix and nine components of final demand (seven consumer goods, exports and exogeneous demand). Matrix G is given in Appendix 7. We then aggregated these fifty-one sectors into five groups according to the following classification:

1 *private sector*: corresponds to items 1 to 37, 39 to 43, 45, 46 and 48 of the input–output matrix;
2 *public firms selling their production*: items 38 and 44;
3 *imports*: item 51;
4 *public administrations*: items 49 and 50;
5 *rents*: item 47.

Summing over the corresponding lines of matrix G yields the transition coefficients for these five groups (see Table 4.7).

We have plotted on Figures 4.3 to 4.5 the observed and computed levels of imports and of the value added by the private sector and by public firms.

Although (4.10) yields a satisfactory approximation of the evolution of imports and value added, it appears that the analysis should be further refined. The fitted and actual values are quite close to one another around 1975, but the difference between these two values increases during periods more remote from the year of reference.

Let us also note that the value added by both the public administrations and 'rents' do not involve a production process which may be influenced by variations in the tax rates on consumer goods. We thus no longer feel

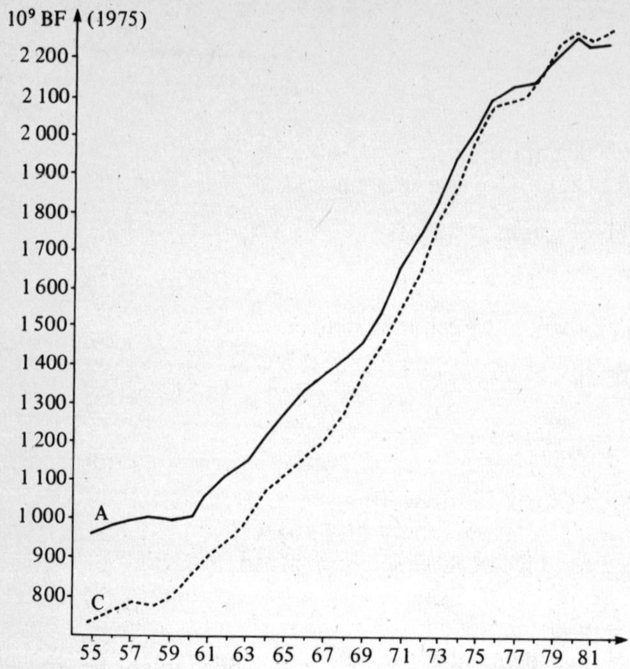

Figure 4.3 Value added of private sector: actual (A) and computed (C)

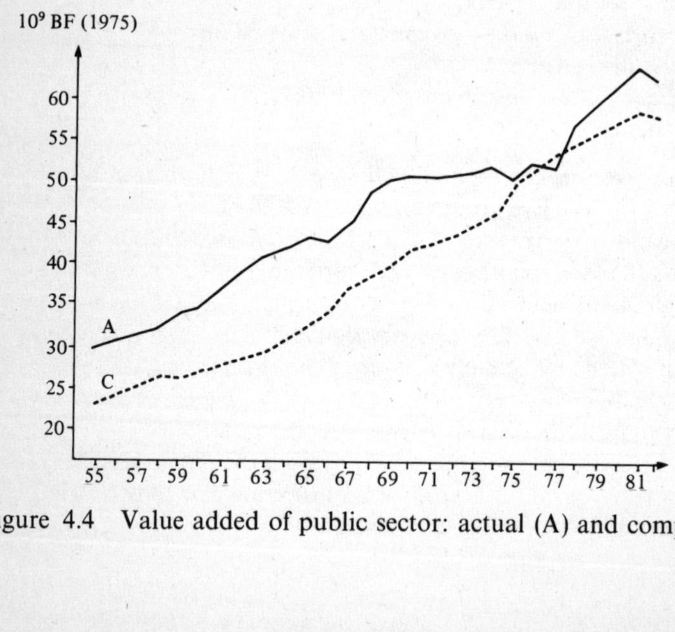

Figure 4.4 Value added of public sector: actual (A) and computed (C)

inclined to model the behaviour of these two sectors. We shall therefore limit ourselves to adding, according to (4.13), an error term to the import equation and to the private and public production sectors equations.

It is assumed that the observed values of imports and value added are proportional to those computed by (4.10), or more formally

$$V_{it} = K_i \hat{V}_{it}, \tag{4.14}$$

where V_{it} is the value added at time t in sector i (i = private sector, public sector, imports),
$\hat{V}_{it}$ is the value computed by (4.10) for sector i at time t,
K_i is the proportionality factor which may vary with the rate of growth of V_{it}.

The fact that K_i is not constant simulates the hypothesis that the coefficients of matrix G may vary in time.

If we let lower-case letters express the logarithm of the corresponding variable, (4.14) can be rewritten as

$$v_{it} = k_i + \hat{v}_{it} \tag{4.15}$$

or passing to first differences

$$\Delta v_{it} = \Delta \hat{v}_{it}. \tag{4.15'}$$

The last two equations characterise a state which might be labelled as 'stationary' or of 'stable evolution'. To explain variations around this trend, we would like to define a relationship of 'disequilibrium' between v_{it} and $\hat{v}_{it}$ which reproduces (4.14) at the stationary state. Such a process is typical of the so-called Error Correction Mechanism (see Davidson *et al.*, 1978).

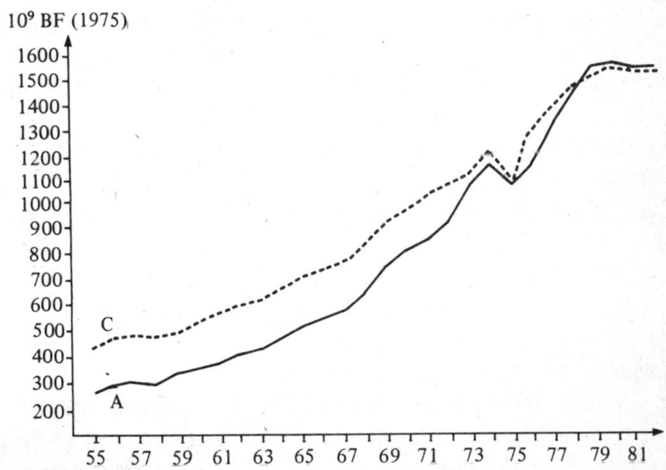

Figure 4.5 Imports: actual (A) and computed (C)

Let us first assume that v_{it} follows a dynamic process of the general form

$$v_{it} = \beta_{0i} + \beta_{1i}\hat{v}_{it} + \beta_{2i}\hat{v}_{it-1} + \beta_{3i}v_{it-1} + e_{it} \tag{4.16}$$

where $e_{it} \sim N(0, \sigma_i^2)$.

For (4.16) to reproduce (4.14) at the stationary state, the following restriction must be imposed

$$\beta_{1i} + \beta_{2i} + \beta_{3i} = 1, \quad \forall i. \tag{4.17}$$

Combining (4.16) and (4.17), one obtains

$$\Delta v_{it} = \beta_{0i} + \beta_{1i}\Delta\hat{v}_{it} + (1 - \beta_{3i})(\hat{v}_{it-1} - v_{it-1}) + e_{it}. \tag{4.18}$$

The stochastic disequilibrium effect is thus represented by $(\hat{v}_{it-1} - v_{it-1})$. Now, if the expansion path at the stationary state is characterised by

$$\Delta v_{it} = g_i = \Delta\hat{v}_{it},$$

then, for $e_{it} = 0$, one has

$$g_i = \frac{\beta_{0i}}{1 - \beta_{1i}} + \frac{(1 - \beta_{3i})}{1 - \beta_{1i}}(\hat{v}_{it-1} - v_{it-1}). \tag{4.19}$$

For $\beta_{3i} \neq 1$, one obtains

$$V_{it} = K_i\hat{V}_{it} \tag{4.20}$$

where $K_i = \exp[(\beta_{0i} - g_i)(1 - \beta_{1i})/(1 - \beta_{3i})]$.

It should be noted that the above analysis does not impose any restriction on the constant term β_{0i} so that (4.16) may be written without it.

To sum up, the error correction mechanism provides us with a link between the observed values of imports and value added and those computed by means of the transition matrix G. The model relies on the hypothesis that there is a variable and proportional relationship between V_{it} and $\hat{V}_{it}$ and explains the observed deviations with respect to the general trend by a factor of 'disequilibrium' equal to $(\hat{v}_{it-1} - v_{it-1})$.

The results obtained from the estimation of (4.18) over the period 1955–1982 are given in Table 4.8.

We must however ascertain that the restriction (4.17) is not too constraining and we therefore estimated (4.16) for the three sectors without imposing any constraint on the parameters. The results of these unrestricted estimations are given in Table 4.9.

These results are highly satisfactory since in all three cases, the sum of the coefficients is not significantly different from 1 at the level of 95 per cent. This suggests that the equations naturally follow an error correction mechanism pattern.

Table 4.8. *Estimation of* (4.18)

	β_{1i}	$(1-\beta_{3i})$	$D-W$	$\hat{\sigma}$
Private sector	0.770	0.006	2.020	0.010
	(0.060)	(0.022)		
Public sector	0.989	0.025	1.980	0.030
	(0.240)	(0.049)		
Imports	1.614	0.003	1.970	0.026
	(0.140)	(0.021)		

Table 4.9. *Unrestricted estimations of* (4.16)

	β_{1i}	β_{2i}	β_{3i}	$D-W$	$\hat{\sigma}$
Private sector	0.780	−0.800	1.012	2.070	0.010
	(0.076)	(0.070)	(0.027)		
Public sector	0.938	−0.880	0.940	1.950	0.030
	(0.260)	(0.250)	(0.073)		
Imports	1.700	−1.690	0.988	1.920	0.026
	(0.160)	(0.170)	(0.025)		

When simulating our tax reform model, we shall therefore estimate the impact on production of variations in the final demand items in two stages: the first consists in a crude estimate obtained by means of the coefficients of the transition matrix G. Secondly, the final impact on imports and value added will be computed by applying the error correction process (4.18). The values forecasted may then be used to derive the induced variations in profits and labour requirements.[3]

4.5 The demand for labour

To estimate the short-run elasticities of the demand for labour in the private sector with respect to wages and output, we follow Drèze and Modigliani (1981) who, by averaging estimates obtained in several existing models of the Belgian economy, conclude that these elasticities can be respectively set at −0.2 and 0.32.

[3] We fully realise that some ambiguity is introduced when considering a transition matrix based on the coefficients of the input–output matrix on the one hand, and an 'independent' labour demand function derived from another production process on the other hand. This dichotomy is due to our desire to estimate the elasticity of labour demand, not only with respect to output, but also with respect to wages. The latter cannot be computed in a production framework characterised by fixed technical coefficients (i.e., which assumes fixed relative production prices), hence the necessity to estimate an autonomous labour demand function.

On the other hand, the public production sector in Belgium sells essentially transportation and communication services. We assume that this sector does not attempt to maximise profits and that it faces a Cobb–Douglas production function. The demand for labour is thus expressed as

$$\log l_t^{z*} = \frac{\log A}{\alpha} + \frac{1}{\alpha}\log z_t - \frac{\beta}{\alpha}\log k_t - \frac{\gamma}{\alpha}t \tag{4.21}$$

where l_t^{z*} is the optimal amount of labour needed to produce output z_t,
k_t is the stock of capital at time t,
t is a trend variable representing technological progress.

It is also assumed that this demand for labour follows a partial adjustment mechanism of the form

$$\left(\frac{l_t^z}{l_{t-1}^z}\right) = \left(\frac{l_t^{z*}}{l_{t-1}^z}\right)^\lambda, \quad 0 < \lambda \leqslant 1. \tag{4.22}$$

Finally, since data on k_t are not available, we suppose that the effect of capital substitution is represented by the trend variable. Hence, substituting (4.22) into (4.21) yields

$$\log l_t^z = \delta_0 + \delta_1 \log z_t + \lambda\delta_2 t + (1-\lambda)\log l_{t-1}^z + \varepsilon_t. \tag{4.23}$$

Estimation of this latter relationship by OLS over the period 1961–1982 yields[4]

$$\begin{aligned} \log l_t^z = \underset{(2.78)}{1.78} + \underset{(0.167)}{0.075}\log z_t - \underset{(0.0005)}{0.00005}t + \underset{(0.189)}{0.833}\log l_{t-1}^z + e_t \end{aligned} \tag{4.24}$$

$$R^2 = 0.866.$$

We note the inertia characterising the adjustment process ($\lambda = 0.17$) and the very low elasticity of demand for labour with respect to value added. These results should not surprise us since we are dealing with public services which, institutionally, have little flexibility in their employment policy.

4.6 Conclusions

In this chapter, we estimated the various relations needed to compute a vector (∂S_K) for the Belgian economy. Some of the results have been borrowed from existing models (such as the elasticity of exports to wages

[4] The estimation concerns the following firms: R.T.T., Régie des Postes, S.N.C.B., S.N.C.V., M.I.V.G., M.I.V.A., S.T.I.V., S.T.I.L., S.T.I.C. and S.T.I.B. Data on value added emanate from the National Accounts and those on labour from Robert *et al.* (1983).

and the elasticities of labour demand in the private sector to wages and production); those that were estimated here seem to be reliable and may be used without too much fear of making dramatic mistakes when actually estimating (∂S_K).

However, we should point out again the hypothesis made at the beginning of this chapter which stated that the whole Belgian economy was operating in an Keynesian context in 1982. Let us repeat that such an assumption can only be accepted in view of the relatively small proportion of firms that were then in another regime. If this proportion were to increase it is clear that we should do away with this assumption and adapt our analysis accordingly. More specifically, the 'linkage' between the production and the consumption sectors, which in our study is based on the input–output framework, would have to be modified. Indeed, and as shown by Lambert (1986), the traditional input–output multiplier analysis implicitly assumes a pure Keynesian regime to prevail for the whole economy and is hence no longer valid once we depart from this assumption.

This situation is far from being desperate since Lambert proposes an 'aggregation by integration approach' in which each sector is considered to be composed of many micro-markets in different disequilibrium regimes. From these considerations, Lambert derives a general formulation for the input–output analysis for a 'mixed' disequilibrium economy, i.e.,

$$\Delta S = [(I - MA)^{-1}M]\Delta F^d, \tag{4.25}$$

where M is a diagonal matrix whose typical element m_{ii} is equal to $(1 - P_i)^{v_i}$ where P_i designates the proportion of micro markets of sector i in excess demand and v_i is a function of the dispersion of demands versus supplies at the micro level.

As for the estimation of the elements of matrix M, the proportion of micro-markets in excess demand can be determined for each sector by the business survey mentioned above, whereas the dispersion of demands versus supplies has to be estimated for each sector, which might be more cumbersome.

It is easily seen that (4.25) reproduces (4.6) when the economy is fully Keynesian since, in that case, all the P_i's are equal to zero and consequently M reduces to the identity matrix. As in 1982 the number of firms in excess supply was fairly small in nearly all the sectors of the economy and, since, as we shall see in the next chapter, the tax directions advocated imply very little change in final demand, we have the feeling that, in our case, the computation of matrix M is not worth its cost.

5 Computation of Pareto improving directions

In the first section of this chapter, we estimate, using the results of Chapter 4, the global effect of a general tax increase on the public sector finances (i.e., vector (∂S_K) as defined by (2.41)). The next step consists in building the consumption cone Λ_K (see (2.42)); this simple but nonetheless crucial problem is taken over in Section 5.2.

Finally, in Section 5.3, we compute several Pareto improving directions of tax reform and estimate the measure of the set of admissible solutions.

5.1 Construction of (∂S_K)

With the results obtained in the previous chapter, we are in possession of all the elements necessary to compute the impact on the public sector's budget of a variation of the tax vector. In Table 5.1, one finds the taxation rates of the various consumer goods under consideration.

The high taxation rate of 'food' is easily explained since this item also covers consumption of tobacco and alcohol which are heavily taxed (see also Appendix 8). The item 'communications', on the other hand, concerns for a small part private communication services (e.g., taxis and coach-services) and for its major part goods sold by public firms whose prices are 100 percent revenue for the public sector.

As for wages, the government has two instruments at its disposal as it may induce variations in the net wage rate either by adapting the tax scale or by modifying the social security contribution rates. At the end of 1982, the standard rate of social contribution borne by the workers represented 10.82 percent of the gross wage (this rate applied only to private sector workers: the situation was much more intricate in the public sector). Gross wages minus these social contributions constitute taxable labour income which in 1982 reached 1630 billions BF. Of this sum 445 billions, i.e. 27.2 percent, were paid in taxes (see I.N.S., 1984). We shall not specify here which one of these two instruments the public sector uses in the tax reform since its choice does not affect the net final results.

Table 5.1. *Taxation rates and consumption levels in 1982*

	Tax in %	Consumption in 1982 ($\times 10^9$ BF)
Food	14.17	627.8
Durables	10.76	433.8
Energy	32.80	255.3
Housing	3.51	395.6
Services	8.83	475.5
Communications	83.12	50.5
Clothing	15.36	192.2

Table 5.2. *Simulation of a 1% price increase*

Variation in consumption	0.065%
Variation in value added (private sector)	−0.001%
Variation in value added (public sector)	0.003%
Variation in employment	−0.15%
Variation in government income	4.19 × 10⁹ BF
Variation in profits	−5.100%
(∂S) vector	
	Effect on budget
Variation of 1% in the price of	($\times 10^9$ BF)
food	3.56
durables	2.47
energy	1.46
housing	2.33
services	2.66
communications	0.31
clothing	1.16
labour	−9.76

In Table 5.2, we give the results obtained by increasing all prices – including net wages – by 1 percent. These increases are expressed in corresponding variations of the taxation rate; since $q_i = (1 + t_i)p_i$ and $dq_i/q_i = 0.01$, we have $dt_i = (q_i/p_i)(0.01)$.

These results suggest that overall consumption increases only very slightly which might seem surprising as income is indexed and net wages are increased by 1 percent. But it should be remembered that (i) nearly 30 percent of total income is not affected by the indexation scheme (capital and self-employed income); (ii) the increase of revenue resulting from the indexation is, as said before, taxed at a marginal rate of 45 percent, and (iii) the impact of the 1 percent wage increase is somewhat limited as net

Table 5.3. *Households' characteristics*

characteristics deciles	1	2	3	4	5	6	7	8	9	10
Disposable income (BF)	171,541	270,739	348,663	416,209	486,045	555,656	625,792	704,682	815,619	1,203,589
Share of labour income (%)	4.00	6.00	20.90	41.00	49.10	62.00	64.90	66.30	61.80	48.40
dividends	0.03	0.23	0.60	0.20	0.05	0.03	0.07	0.02	0.60	0.26
unemployment benefits	2.90	2.20	2.60	3.60	3.20	4.80	2.40	2.50	2.00	0.40
pensions	72.40	64.40	44.40	27.50	16.45	9.40	5.50	5.20	4.40	2.30
other sources	20.67	27.17	31.50	27.70	31.20	23.77	27.13	25.98	31.20	48.64
Consumption (% of total)										
food	31.30	29.46	27.70	26.80	26.20	23.30	23.20	21.60	20.20	17.50
durables	4.40	5.60	7.25	10.50	10.00	13.10	14.50	13.40	14.50	15.90
energy	12.20	11.30	10.10	10.10	9.80	9.40	0.70	0.60	8.70	8.06
housing	25.70	24.90	22.90	20.80	20.90	18.50	17.30	19.50	19.60	21.30
communication	1.91	2.10	2.20	1.80	1.90	2.10	1.80	1.70	2.10	1.90
clothing	5.43	6.30	6.80	7.60	8.10	8.20	9.10	8.90	8.50	8.50
services	19.40	20.40	23.20	22.60	23.10	25.60	24.20	25.70	26.70	27.40

labour revenues constitute only about 50 percent of total disposable income. This explains why the joint effect of the indexation process and of the rise in net wages are just sufficient to compensate for the general increase in prices.

The decrease in the value added of the private sector is explained by the drop in exports caused by the indexation of wages. The loss of foreign markets and the rise in the wage bill underlie the sharp decrease in employment and profits.

The increase in the value added of the public sector is so small that it adds very little to government income. The positive effect on the public sector's budget results essentially from the increase in the price of food, durables, housing and services.

The impact of the 1 percent increase in net wages (i.e., a net cost to the state of 9.76 billions out of an initial decrease in taxes of approximately 12 billion francs) can be compared to a simulation carried out by the Bureau du Plan with the MARIBEL model (Bureau du Plan, 1985). In this exercise, the Bureau du Plan forecasted that a 40 billion francs decrease in income tax in 1986 would result in a net loss of 35.9 billions for the public sector. These results differ little from our own, which leaves us somewhat reassured as to the reliability of our model.

5.2 Construction of Λ_K

To estimate the elements (∂C_K^h) of the cone Λ_K) of the cone Λ_K (see (2.40) and (2.42)), we used the results of a survey on household budgets carried out in 1978–79 (see I.N.S., 1984) on a sample of 2,443 households; these are classified into deciles according to disposable income and characterised by their consumption bundle, labour supply and sources of income. We corrected however these data by introducing coefficients allowing for tax evasion. These were borrowed from Meulders and Tollet (1975). We also assumed that the distribution of consumption, income, share in profits and unemployment benefits across the deciles remained constant between 1979 and 1982 in order to obtain a hopefully reliable estimation of a vector (∂C_K^h) for each of the ten deciles (see Table 5.3).

These estimations call for several comments. First, the households which are the most affected by variations in the wage rate are concentrated in the upper half of the income classes. The two lowest deciles are hardly affected by such changes as the share of labour revenue in their total disposable income lies between 4 and 6 percent. The source of income of these households basically consists of social benefits (old-age and invalidity pensions) which are not controlled in our model but which are however linked to the evolution of consumer prices through the indexation process.

Table 5.4. *Unemployment per household*

Deciles	1	2	3	4	5	6	7	8	9	10
Average number of persons per household	1.4	1.9	2.1	2.5	3.0	3.2	3.6	3.7	3.7	4.3
Number of unemployed per decile in the sample	8	10	13	11	23	36	19	22	16	10
of which:										
1st member	6	5	6	5	1	7	2	2	3	0
2nd member	1	4	4	4	17	20	14	15	10	4
3rd member	1	1	2	2	5	6	1	4	3	2
4th and over	0	0	1	0	0	3	2	1	0	4
Share of unemployment with respect to total (in %)	4.7	5.9	7.8	6.6	13.7	21.4	11.3	13.1	9.5	6.0

The data on consumption are relatively consonant with common intuition: the share of durables, clothing and services (which includes leisure) in total expenditure increases with income whilst those of food and energy are inversely related to revenue. On the other hand, the share of communication is almost constant across deciles whilst that of housing reaches a peak in the first decile (necessity good), a low in the seventh and goes up again in the last ones (luxury good).

Looking at Table 5.4, we note that 60 percent of total unemployment is concentrated between the fifth and eighth deciles. This table makes it also clear that in these income classes unemployment essentially affects the second and the third member of the household (i.e., generally the wife and the eldest child). These statistics suggest, contrary to some common opinion, that a policy seeking to increase employment will not necessarily benefit the poorest households but on the contrary may only result in an increase in income inequality. This observation is but reinforced by our suspicion that lower-income households essentially supply unqualified labour and, as such, are already penalised on the labour market.

We are now left with the question of how to estimate the reservation wage q_R^h appearing in (2.40). Little empirical evidence exists as to plausible values that these parameters could take, and the few surveys concerned with this estimation also sometimes yield contradictory results. We report here of two such surveys which were carried out in the United States.

In the first one, Stephenson (1976) considers a sample of 300 unemployed young males aged from eighteen to twenty-one years, who were seeking full-time jobs through state employment agencies. Each youth had at least been employed once in the past two years. Their answers to the question 'What is the minimum hourly wage rate or weekly take home pay you would accept at present?' were used to estimate the youths' reservation wage. These answers were then compared with the respondent's last wage. For this sample, the relative reservation wage averaged 84 percent.

Feldstein and Poterba (1984), on the other hand, report on a survey conducted by the U.S. Department of Labour in 1976 on a sample of 4,668 unemployed persons. They were asked to fill in a questionnaire concerning their work experience, previous earnings and aspirations. The response rate was 69 percent and, after discarding new entrants on the labour market, the authors examined the answers given by 2,228 unemployed. To the question 'What is the lowest salary you would accept for the job you are looking for?', 31 percent of the job losers answered that they would only work for a wage *higher* than their last one, which implies that these agents were voluntarily unemployed. The mean ratio of the reservation wage to the last wage was 1.03 for job losers and 1.07 for all job losers and leavers. These ratios are surprisingly high and in our opinion should be interpreted with great care. We do not think that these results fit the Belgian situation in 1982, which was characterised by a high rate of unemployment amongst the youngsters (new entrants) and a very low labour mobility, i.e. possible factors of downward pressure on reservation wages. We thus feel inclined to believe that the reservation wage was lower than the market wage. In the remainder of our work we shall hence carry out simulations using different values for the reservation wage, imposing however the ratio q_R^h/q_l^h to be less than unity.

Finally, two concluding remarks should be made about the impact of the classification of households adopted here on the probability of finding PID's.

Firstly, working with deciles implies that one discards extreme households, which is equivalent to 'shrinking' the consumption cone Λ_K. As has already been observed in Section 2.2, this shrinking should increase the chances of finding PID's.

Secondly, one should also bear in mind that the vectors (∂C_K^h) we have just built characterise 'ideal' or average households each of which is at the same time retired, on the dole, a shareholder and a wage-earner! These unnatural characteristics will certainly have a considerable influence on the interpretation of our final results. However, in view of the negligible share of wages in the total income of the two lowest deciles, one could consider these as being representative of fully unemployed households. Since the average annual unemployment benefit in 1982 amounted to approximately 212,000 BF per unemployed (with a minimum of 56,000

Table 5.5. *Solution of programme (5.1): tax directions in %*

q_R^h/q_I^h	0.4	0.52	0.64	0.76	0.88	1.00	1.06–0.06h
Food	−1.294	−1.294	−1.295	−1.296	−1.296	−1.297	−1.296
Durables	0	0	0	0	0	0	0
Energy	2.875	2.876	2.878	2.882	2.882	2.883	2.88
Housing	0	0	0	0	0	0	0
Services	−1.117	−1.116	−1.116	−1.117	−1.116	−1.116	−1.116
Communications	4.507	4.506	4.502	4.498	4.497	4.496	4.5
Clothing	0	0	0	0	0	0	0
Labour	−0.206	−0.206	−0.206	−0.206	−0.206	−0.206	−0.206

BF and a maximum of 282,000 BF), the first decile could very well characterise the behaviour of a 'household' composed of one unemployed agent. On the other hand, since the average number of agents in a second decile household is 1.9, the second column of Table 5.2 could be representative of a household composed of one agent of no occupation and of another who is on the dole.

5.3 PID of tax reform

5.3.1 Existence and computation of PID's

Checking whether $\mathring{\Lambda}^*_K \cap S^\perp_K \neq \phi$ can be done by solving a simple linear programme (see Chapter 3). We adopt here the following procedure

$$\begin{aligned}
&\underset{dq}{\text{Min}} \sum_h \lambda^h (\partial C^h_K)' dq && (5.1)\\
&\text{s.t.} \quad (\partial C^h_K)' dq \leqslant 0, \quad h = 1, \ldots, 10\\
&\qquad (\partial S_K)' dq = 0\\
&\qquad \sum_h |dq_i| \leqslant 1.
\end{aligned}$$

Solving (5.1) actually amounts to killing two birds with one stone since, in addition to proving existence, a solution also provides a 'best' direction given the chosen set of λ^h's. In the present case we have defined, rather arbitrarily, λ^h $(h = 1, \ldots, 10)$ as inversely proportional to household h's income.

As is suggested in the previous section, this programme has to be solved for several alternative values of the agents' reservation wage. In an initial series of six simulations, we suppose that the ratio q^h_R/q^h_l lies between 0.4 and 1 and that it is constant across households. We next assume the ratio q^h_R/q^h_l to be a decreasing function of income or equivalently of h. Thus we define $q^h_R/q^h_l = 1.06 - 0.06h$ so that the reservation wage is equal to the wage rate for the first decile but only to 46 percent of this rate for the last decile. The results of these simulations are to be found in Table 5.5. We see that every programme has a feasible solution which is nearly invariant to the value taken by the reservation wage.

We thus feel inclined to acknowledge that PID's do exist and are somewhat reassured since the results of the simulations are hardly affected by the value of the reservation wage.

In Table 5.6, we give the overall effects on the economy caused by the tax variations shown in the last column of Table 5.5.

It is verified that adopting social weights λ^h inversely proportional to disposable income effectively leads to a solution favourable to lower income deciles which may be easily interpreted by going back to the

Table 5.6. *Effects of the tax reform*

Variation of consumption	0.030%
Variation of value added (private sector)	0.023%
Variation of value added (public sector)	−0.190%
Variation of employment	0.029%
Variation of profits	1.260%
Variation of price index	−0.150%

structure of the households' consumption (see Table 5.3). The sharp decrease in food prices benefits essentially the lower deciles since food, together with housing, represent the largest share of their total expenditure. The fall in the tax on services, on the other hand, is far more favourable to middle- and higher-income classes. The increases in the rate of tax on energy and transport services have relatively little impact on utility since the share of these items in total expenditure is small. The general price decrease involves, through the indexation process, a fall in the gross wage rate which in turn causes profits and employment to increase. Higher profits improve mainly the higher deciles' utility, while the creation of new jobs improves that of the middle deciles which are the most affected by unemployment (see Table 5.4). Finally, the drop in the net wage rate hardly affects the lower deciles who derive the main share of their income from social benefits.

These economic changes may however be undesirable at a more disaggregate level. Indeed, the decrease in net wages linked with an increase in profits and employment could be unsatisfactory for a non-shareholder worker. But this cannot be captured in a model assuming 'ideal' households – or deciles – which are all affected by variations in the level of employment and profits. In the remainder of this section, we therefore try to work out more flexible policies.

In a first attempt, we solve programme (5.1) with the additional constraint that the labour income tax cannot be increased (i.e.: $dq_l \geqslant 0$). The solution to this new problem with $q_R^h/q_l^h = 1.06 - 0.06h$ is shown in Table 5.7.

The tax direction advocated by this experiment is in fact not too different from the previous one. Prices move in the same direction except, naturally, for wages which reach their lower bound. Not surprisingly, the impact on the economy of these movements is not too different from that of the previous one and the same kind of comments therefore applies.

A second attempt to generalise our results consists in doubling the number of households by assuming that each decile is represented by a household constrained on the labour market and another which is not. Both types of households are assumed to have the same consumption

Table 5.7. *Programme* (*5.1*) *with* $dq_l \geqslant 0$

Food	−0.98%
Durables	0%
Energy	1.18%
Housing	0%
Services	−1.07%
Communications	3.77%
Clothing	2.99%
Labour	0%
Variation in consumption	0.03%
Variation in employment	0.01%
Variation in profits	0.40%
Variation in prices	−0.25%

Table 5.8. *Solution of* (*5.1*) *with 20 agents*

Food	−1.30%
Durables	0%
Energy	2.89%
Housing	0%
Services	−1.11%
Communications	4.47%
Clothing	0%
Labour	0.21%

structure as shown in Table 5.3. But, whereas the income structure of the labour-constrained households is the same as in the previous experiments, it is assumed that the term $\frac{dl}{dq}$ no longer appears in the vector (∂C_K^h)'s characterising the unconstrained agents. The results of this simulation (keeping $q_R^h/q_l^h = 1.06 - 0.06h$) are given in Table 5.8 and differ very little from those of the original experiment (see Table 5.5). This can be explained by the fairly small impact on employment $\left(\text{i.e., on } \frac{dl}{dq}\right)$ of the advocated tax direction vector.

In a final attempt to test the sensitivity of our results to the specification of the vectors (∂C_K^h)'s, we transformed the data concerning households. As was noted in Section 5.2, the first decile may be assimilated to a fully unemployed agent. Accordingly, we transformed the vector (∂C_K^1) so as to make it totally independent of variations in net wages and profits.

Table 5.9. *Programme (5.1) with transformed data*

Food	−1.55%
Durables	0%
Energy	2.50%
Housing	0.69%
Services	1.52%
Communications	0%
Clothing	3.71%
Labour	0%
Variation in consumption	0.07%
Variation in employment	0.01%
Variation in profits	0.06%
Variation in prices	−0.03%

Moreover, it is assumed that this household cannot be affected by changes in the employment level. In other words, we impose that this agent remains unemployed whatever happens on the labour market. At the same time, we suppose that the ninth agent is fully employed and a non-shareholder while the tenth household is also fully employed, but remains a recipient of capital income. Looking back at formula (2.40), this amounts to saying that (i) $\frac{dl}{dq} = 0$ for (∂C_K^1), (∂C_K^9) and (∂C_K^{10}), (ii) θ^1 and θ^9 equal zero, and (iii) the last component of (∂C_K^1) also equals zero. Solving (5.1) with this new set of data yields the results given in Table 5.9.

This solution is probably the most satisfactory of all those we have obtained so far. It is characterised by an increase in employment, consumption and profits and it leaves all the agents better off, even the poorest one who stays on the dole.

Our enthusiasm should however be curbed by the fact that the reform advocated implies very small changes in the macroeconomic aggregates. Indeed, if we take the maximum magnitude allowed by these tax directions before a commodity has to be subsidised (namely multiplying the direction of Table 5.9 by a factor of approximately six, hence involving a zero-tax on services (see also Table 5.1)), we obtain the results given in Table 5.10.

Although the price variations are now considerable, not to say huge (20 percent change in the price of clothing!), their impact on overall consumption and employment remains almost negligible. As is easily seen, the same kind of procedure, carried out with the directions obtained in the previous simulations, also results in very little modifications in the main macroeconomic aggregates. We can therefore conclude that, although PID's of tax reform seemed to exist in Belgium in 1982, the

Table 5.10. *Effect of 'maximum' dq*

Food	−9.30%
Durables	0%
Energy	15.00%
Housing	4.14%
Services	−9.12%
Communications	0%
Clothing	22.6%
Labour	0%
Variation in consumption	0.44%
Variation in employment	0.08%
Variation in profits	0.33%
Variation in prices	0.17%

implementation of these directions may not have helped to boost the economy. We shall come back to this point in our final conclusions.

Finally, and again in order to generalise our results, we endeavoured to build the whole set of PID's, i.e. the cone $\mathring{\Lambda}_K^* \cap S_K^\perp$. A generator of a convex cone in $\mathbb{R}^m$ is defined as the intersection of $(m-1)$ hyperplanes. In our case we have eleven constraints (ten on the households' utility and one on the public sector budget) in eight unknowns (since we have eight instruments). We should thus solve every sub-system of seven equations and check whether the solution verifies the four remaining constraints (there are $\binom{11}{7}$ such systems). But the number of combinations to be examined can be somewhat reduced since the solution has to lie on $S_K^\perp$. Hence, we only have to select six equations out of the ten defined by $(\partial C_K^h)'dq \leqslant 0 \quad (h = 1, \ldots, 10)$ and solve these with the additional $(\partial S_K)'dq = 0$. We thus have $\binom{10}{6} = 210$ systems to examine. The set of solutions defined by these systems comprises all the generators of $S_K^\perp \cap \Lambda_K^*$. Taking the sets H_i's $(i = 1, \ldots, 210)$ of six indices chosen out of ten, the 210 following linear programmes have to be solved

$$\min_{dq} (\partial C_K^l)'dq \qquad \text{for any} \quad l \notin H_i, \quad i = 1, \ldots, 210 \tag{5.2}$$

$$\begin{aligned} \text{s.t.} \quad & (\partial S_K)'dq = 0 \\ & (\partial C_K^h)'dq = 0, \quad \forall h \in H_i \\ & (\partial C_K^k)'dq \leqslant 0, \quad \forall k \notin H_i \\ & \sum_j |dq_j| \leqslant 1. \end{aligned}$$

Fifty-six of these systems yielded an optimal solution different from zero. It had to be verified though that some of these vectors were not positive linear combinations of other solutions. Twenty-three vectors were eliminated on this ground so that eventually we concluded that $S_K^{\perp} \cap \Lambda_K^*$ is generated by the thirty-three vectors of tax direction shown in Appendix 9. Every positive linear combination of these vectors yields a Pareto Improving Direction of tax reform.

Finally, we wished to compute the probability that a tax direction leaving the public sector's budget unaffected also improves the agents' utility. This was achieved by a Monte-Carlo procedure consisting in generating pseudo-random vectors in $S_K^{\perp}$. The ratio of the number of vectors included in Λ_K^* to the total number of directions generated provides us with an approximation of the desired probability.

One million such vectors were generated and 6,067 of them happened to lie in Λ_K^* (i.e., a success rate of 0.006067 with a standard-error of 0.000077). We can therefore say that, if the public sector chooses a tax direction $dq \in S_K^{\perp}$, it has approximately six chances in a thousand of improving every agent's utility.

5.3.2 *Welfare and inequality aversion*

Since empirical evidence suggests that PID's of tax reform exist for our set of data, we can now test whether the solution to programme (5.1) is sensitive to changes in the specification of the social welfare function, i.e. to variations in the social weights λ^h's. There are numerous ways of defining these but, as suggested by Ahmad and Stern (1984), an interesting specification is obtained by adopting the following utility functions with respect to income

$$\begin{aligned} u^h(I^h) &= k(I^h)^{1-e}(1-e)^{-1} \qquad \text{if} \quad e \neq 1, \quad e \geqslant 0 \qquad (5.3) \\ &= k \log (I^h) \qquad \text{if} \quad e = 1. \end{aligned}$$

where I^h is agent h's disposable income
k is a constant
$e \geqslant 0$ for concavity.

If we let $k = (I^1)^{1/e}(1-e)$, with I^1 the poorest household's income, we obtain

$$\lambda^h = \frac{\partial u^h(I^h)}{\partial I^h} = \left(\frac{I^1}{I^h}\right)^e. \qquad (5.4)$$

λ^h represents the marginal social value of a unit of income to h relative to a unit of income to agent 1 (as seen from the public sector's viewpoint). Since this measure is an increasing function in e, this parameter can be considered as an indicator of inequality aversion. Indeed setting $e = 0$ gives the same weight to every agent, while for higher values of e we approach Rawlsian-type utility functions, i.e. which makes the worst off best off. In our case, and since the tenth agent's income is seven times that of the first agent (see Table 5.3), taking $e = 5$ would mean that a marginal increase in the welfare of the poorest is 7^5 (= 16,807) times worth that in the welfare of the richest. The exercise consists now in solving programme (5.1) with the social welfare weights defined in (5.4) and for several values of e.

We present the tax directions advocated for $e = (0, 0.1, 0.5, 1, 2, 3, 4, 5)$ and the welfare gain for each household associated with these directions in Tables 5.11 and 5.12 respectively. From these results, we see that the inequality coefficient plays its role in a step-wise fashion. With $e < 1$, and, even if the tax on food decreases, the tax variations are relatively unfavourable to the lower deciles as energy and housing are getting dearer. With $e = 1$, the tax on housing stays unchanged and for higher values of inequality aversion the message is quite clear: decrease slightly the taxes on *all* the poorer households' main expenditure items and increase sharply those on communication services and clothing which together represent only 7.3 percent of the first decile's total expenditure.

These results do not suggest the existence of a systematic path leading to the levying of higher taxes on already heavily taxed goods or on the contrary, to a more uniform tax system. The fact that we do not find such a clear pattern here is most probably due to our not requiring to leave anyone worse off in the tax reform process. In other words, constraining each individual's utility may have led to results which are somewhat less predictable than those we would have obtained if we had merely adopted the strategy of a collectively increasing tax reform.

In the next stage we abandon the Paretian criterion, i.e. we do not impose everyone to be at least as well off after the tax reform as before. In practice, we no longer require the two last deciles' utility to increase in the tax reform process. This was achieved by solving programme (5.1) but by discarding the constraints on (∂C_K^9) and (∂C_K^{10}).

The results of this simulation are given in Table 5.13.

It appears that the whole weight of the utility increasing aspect of the reform is borne by a sharp decrease in the price of food. On the other hand, a significant increase in the tax on housing, combined with a small rise in the tax on durables and labour, is needed to balance the public sector's accounts.

5.3.3 *Maximisation of* (∂S_K)

Our last experiment consists in determining the tax direction which maximises (∂S_K) while leaving no one worse off. This means that we are

Table 5.11. *Tax directions as function of inequality aversion*

e	0	0.1	0.5	1	2	3	4	5
Food	−0.177	−0.177	−0.177	−0.129	−0.123	−0.121	−0.077	−0.077
Durables	0	0	0	0	0	−0.003	−0.037	−0.037
Energy	0.404	0.404	0.404	0.288	0.274	0.267	0	0
Housing	0.116	0.116	0.116	0	−0.008	−0.012	−0.043	−0.043
Services	−0.179	−0.179	−0.179	−0.111	−0.104	−0.097	−0.025	−0.025
Communications	0.100	0.100	0.100	0.450	0.468	0.470	0.320	0.320
Clothing	0	0	0	0	0	0	0.480	0.480
Labour	−0.022	−0.022	−0.022	−0.020	−0.020	−0.019	0.012	0.012

Table 5.12. *Welfare variations (BF per household per year)*

deciles	*e* 0	0.1	0.5	1	2	3	4	5
1	0	0	0	195	206	213	288	288
2	295	295	295	430	435	435	270	270
3	636	636	636	603	594	580	268	268
4	457	457	457	467	460	457	348	348
5	427	427	427	386	377	370	237	237
6	560	560	560	244	217	203	217	217
7	244	244	244	168	0	0	0	0
8	0	0	0	0	0	0	0	0
9	286	286	286	295	10	0	0	0
10	0	0	0	0	0	0	0	0

Table 5.13. *Programme (5.1) without constraint on the last two deciles*

Food	−4.12%
Durables	0.74%
Energy	0%
Housing	5.00%
Services	0%
Communications	0%
Clothing	0%
Labour	−0.12%
Variation in consumption	0.09%
Variation in employment	0.03%
Variation in profits	1.30%
Variation in prices	−0.11%

no longer looking for PID's in a strict sense as we are prepared to create a surplus on the government's side which otherwise could have been redistributed in order to increase welfare. However, in these times of high deficits, this approach cannot be ignored and, on the contrary, should actually be cherished by destitute governments. Accordingly, the following programme has to be solved

$$\max_{dq} (\partial S_K)' dq \tag{5.5}$$

$$\text{s.t.} \quad (\partial C_K^h)' dq \leqslant 0, \quad \forall h$$

$$\sum_i |dq_i| \leqslant 1.$$

Table 5.14. *Solution to programme (5.5)*

Food	−1.35%
Durables	−1.88%
Energy	1.46%
Housing	1.37%
Services	0%
Communications	3.50%
Clothing	0%
Labour	−0.34%
Variation in consumption	−0.003%
Variation in employment	0.035%
Variation in profits	1.500%
Variation in prices	−0.230%
Variation in State's income	0.360 Billions

The results of this maximisation are shown in Table 5.14 and are essentially characterised by increases in the tax on energy, housing and in particular communications and a decrease in the net wage rate. On the other hand, these utility deteriorating moves are compensated by lower taxes on food and durables.

The solution to programme (5.5) hardly affects overall consumption, but induces higher levels of profits and employment. These can mainly be attributed to the decrease in the wage bill caused by the fall in consumer prices.

However, and in order to corroborate the findings of Sub-Section 5.3.1, we should note that the multiplication of the tax direction shown in Table 5.14 by a factor of 5 (i.e., the maximum of the tax variation we may impose before having to subsidise durables), again results in very small modifications in the main macroeconomic aggregates.

As may be seen in Table 5.15, the main beneficiaries of this tax direction are the middle-class households. Let us recall that it is also in these classes that unemployment is largely concentrated (see Table 5.4).

Finally, we estimated, by means of a Monte-Carlo experiment similar to that of Sub-Section 5.3.1, the joint probability of finding a tax direction which would increase both the public sector's income and the agents' utilities. We generated one million pseudo-random vectors in the sphere of unit radius in R^8, and 1,497 of these satisfied the constraints $(\partial S_K)'dq \geqslant 0$ and $(\partial C_K^h)'dq \leqslant 0$ $(h = 1, \ldots, 10)$, i.e. a joint probability of 0.001497 with a standard-error of 0.000038. We also estimated, again using Monte-Carlo methods, that the measure of Λ^* is equal to 0.007949 (standard-error after generating 10^6 vectors: 0.0000888). From these

Table 5.15. *Welfare variations induced by (5.5)*

Decile	Variation
1	0
2	30
3	84
4	412
5	0
6	374
7	594
8	0
9	122
10	0

Table 5.16. *Probability of the inclusion of dq in $\tilde{S}_K$ and Λ_K^**

$Pr(dq \in \Lambda_K^* \mid dq \in S_K^\perp)$	0.006
$Pr(dq \in \tilde{S}_K, dq \in \Lambda_K^*)$	0.001
$Pr(dq \in \Lambda_K^*)$	0.008
$Pr(dq \in \tilde{S}_K \mid dq \in \Lambda_K^*)$	0.190

probabilities, it can be deduced that the conditional probability of having $(\partial S_K)'dq \geqslant 0$ given $dq \in \Lambda_K^*$ is approximately equal to 0.19 (see Table 5.16).

The cone Λ_K^* is thus divided into two unequal parts, the set of PID's which improves the public sector's finances being four times smaller than that which increases the deficit.

This means that, although the perpendicular hyperplane to (∂S_K) is not 'right in the middle' of Λ_K^*, the margin of manoeuvre left with the public sector is relatively large. This result also insures us against the effects of estimation errors in some – or all! – of the components of the vector (∂S_K). Indeed, such errors should be relatively large before the intersection between Λ_K^* and $S_K^\perp$ vanishes.

5.4 Concluding remarks

In this chapter, after having estimated vector (∂S_K) and the consumption cone Λ_K we computed that the conditions for the existence of PID's obtained in Belgium in 1982; this result is practically invariant to the value taken by the unobservable parameter of our model, i.e., the reservation wage. Several improving directions of tax reform have actually been computed and were shown to be relatively sensitive to the value of the inequality aversion parameter chosen by the decision maker. Moreover, all these directions induce very little changes in final demand and employment.

The whole set of PID's has also been built which gives a fairly good idea of the margin of manoeuvre left to the government if it had attempted, in 1982, to increase welfare through fiscal policies.

Conclusions and suggestions for further work

At the end of this work two kinds of conclusions are in order. First, from a methodological point of view, we have succeeded in deriving formulae for the tax reform problem which are 'easily' estimable whatever regime prevails in the economy. The different formulae differ from one another by the way profit- and employment multipliers are defined, but the various parameters needed to compute them can normally be estimated without too much trouble. In the particular case of Belgium, information on consumer behaviour is unfortunately scarce. This implies a limitation in the level of disaggregation of private consumption (see our comments on this point in Chapters 2 and 5) and increases the probability of finding Pareto improving directions of tax reform. Further study should hence try to consider more agents even if this means that the set of Pareto improving directions may shrink and will probably vanish as the number of consumers taken into account increases, which is equivalent to saying that the economy is at a second-best optimum. In this case, the algorithms described in Chapter 3 could be used to determine the social weights which implicitly underlie this optimum.

From a policy viewpoint the main aspect to be noticed from our empirical results is that, even if Pareto improving directions of tax reform could be found in 1982, the tax changes advocated by our various simulations would have implied only marginal variations in final demand and employment. Several reasons may be invoked to explain this fact. The first one that comes to mind is that the then prevailing tax vector was not the result of a poor choice on the decision taker's part even if this choice could have been slightly improved. This confirms the findings of other models of the Belgian economy in which simulations of 'mild' macroeconomic measures (slight decrease in real wages for instance) did not lead in the short run to important variations in employment (see, for instance, Ginsburgh and Vander Heyden, 1985).

Another reason that may be invoked resides in the institutional framework of the Belgian economy, in particular the wage indexation process which applies even if consumer price variations are the result of a tax modification: this cannot but hinder the government's policy. Indeed, and for instance, an increase in the V.A.T. rates leads, through the indexation mechanism, to an increase in the wage bill of both the public and the private production sector. Higher wages in the latter induces a reduction of the labour forcc and consequently an increase in unemployment whose cost is borne by the government. The combination of the increase in unemployment and in the wages of the public sector decreases the fiscal revenue that can be expected from the initial tax increase; thus, in order to yield a given revenue, the government has to levy higher taxes than if no indexation mechanism prevailed.

To the question raised in the introduction to Chapter 4, i.e. whether tax changes could have some effect on unemployment without decreasing each agent's utility, we are therefore tempted to answer negatively. The fact that a tax reform, in its Paretian formulation, induces very little changes in aggregate demand is certainly disappointing but does not however mean that the model presented in the previous chapters is worthless or useless. Quite on the contrary, it is an invitation to every model builder to disaggregate the consumption sector and to consider many consumers in future econometric models. We have shown that this disaggregation can be carried out at relatively little cost so that it nearly becomes a duty for the decision maker to use the whole available set of data concerning consumers in his search for a fairer society.

If the wastage of human resources, i.e. unemployment, presently known in our society cannot be reduced by mere 'mechanical' tax movements, then new lines of investigation have to be opened. Fortunately, times of crisis are often the right times for new ideas to emerge. May the courage and willingness to apply these not become scarce resources. . . .

Appendixes

1 Indirect utility function and labour constraint

For convenience sake we shall work with only one private consumption good X, one good Z produced by the public sector and labour l. We are also uniquely concerned with the demonstration in the classical regime since, as we shall see, this demonstration encompasses the Keynesian case.

Proof We have

$$\text{Max } u^h(x^h, z^h, l^h) \tag{1}$$

$$\begin{aligned} \text{s.t.} \quad & q_x x^h + q_z z^h - q_l l^h = 0 && (-\varphi^h) \\ & x^h = \bar{x}^h && (-\gamma^h) \\ & l^h = \bar{l}^h && (-\psi^h) \end{aligned}$$

(Let us notice that the Keynesian case is considered by discarding the constraint on x^h.)

The indirect utility function for this problem writes down as $V^h(q_x, q_z, q_l, \bar{l}^h, \bar{x}^h)$ and one has

$$\frac{\partial V^h}{\partial q} = \frac{\partial u^h}{\partial z^h}\frac{\partial z^h}{\partial q} = \varphi^h q_z \frac{\partial z^h}{\partial q} \qquad \text{for} \quad q = (q_x, q_z, q_l) \tag{2}$$

$$\frac{\partial V^h}{\partial \bar{x}^h} = \frac{\partial u^h}{\partial \bar{x}^h} + \frac{\partial u^h}{\partial z^h}\frac{\partial z^h}{\partial \bar{x}^h} = \frac{\partial u^h}{\partial x^h} + \varphi^h \frac{\partial z^h}{\partial \bar{x}^h} \tag{3}$$

$$\frac{\partial V^h}{\partial \bar{l}^h} = \frac{\partial u^h}{\partial \bar{l}^h} + \frac{\partial u^h}{\partial z^h}\frac{\partial z^h}{\partial \bar{l}^h} = \frac{\partial u^h}{\partial \bar{l}^h} + \varphi^h \frac{\partial z^h}{\partial \bar{l}^h} \tag{4}$$

Now taking the first derivative of the Lagrangean of (1) with respect to $\bar{x}^h$ and $\bar{l}^h$ yields

$$\frac{\partial \Lambda}{\partial \bar{l}^h} = \frac{\partial u^h}{\partial \bar{l}^h} + \varphi^h q_l - \psi^h = 0 \tag{5}$$

and

$$\frac{\partial \Lambda}{\partial \bar{x}^h} = \frac{\partial u^h}{\partial \bar{x}^h} - \varphi^h q_x - \gamma^h = 0.$$

Combining (5) with (3) and (4) yields

$$\frac{\partial V^h}{\partial \bar{x}^h} = \varphi^h q_z \frac{\partial z^h}{\partial \bar{x}^h} + \gamma^h + \varphi^h q_x$$

$$\frac{\partial V^h}{\partial \bar{l}^h} = \varphi^h q_z \frac{\partial z^h}{\partial \bar{l}^h} + \psi^h - \varphi^h q_l. \tag{6}$$

Let $B = q_x x^h + q_z z^h - q_l l^h$ and $C^h = (x^h, z^h, -l^h)$; one has

$$\frac{\partial B}{\partial q} = C^h + q_z \frac{\partial z^h}{\partial q} = 0$$

$$\frac{\partial B}{\partial \bar{x}^h} = q_x + q_z \frac{\partial z^h}{\partial \bar{x}^h} = 0 \tag{7}$$

$$\frac{\partial B}{\partial \bar{l}^h} = -q_l + q_z \frac{\partial z^h}{\partial \bar{l}^h} = 0.$$

Substituting (7) in (2) and (6) we may write

$$\frac{\partial V^h}{\partial q} = -\varphi^h C^h$$

$$\frac{\partial V^h}{\partial \bar{x}^h} = -\varphi^h q_x + \gamma^h + \varphi^h q_x$$

$$= \gamma^h \tag{8}$$

$$\frac{\partial V^h}{\partial \bar{l}^h} = \varphi^h q_l + \psi^h - \varphi^h q_l$$

$$= \psi^h$$

Q.E.D.

2 Second-best solution in a Keynesian setting

Proof We may take the first partial derivatives of the Langrangean of (2.37)

$$\frac{\partial \Lambda}{\partial r^h} = \mu^h \frac{\partial V^h}{\partial r^h} + v\left(\frac{\partial l^{p'}}{\partial x}\frac{\partial x}{\partial r^h} + \frac{\partial l^z}{\partial^z}\frac{\partial z}{\partial r^h}\right) - \sigma^h$$

$$+ \sum_j \sigma^h \theta^j \frac{\partial \pi}{\partial r^h} + \rho \frac{\partial S}{\partial r^h} = 0, \quad \forall h. \tag{1}$$

Multiplying each of these equations by θ^h and summing, one obtains

$$\sum_h \mu^h\theta^h \frac{\partial V^h}{\partial r^h} + v\left(\frac{\partial l^{p'}}{\partial x}\frac{\partial x}{\partial r} + \frac{\partial l^z}{\partial z}\frac{\partial z}{\partial r}\right) - \sigma\left(1 - \frac{\partial \pi}{\partial r}\right) + \rho\frac{\partial S}{\partial r} = 0 \tag{2}$$

with $\sigma = \sum_j \theta^j\sigma^j$, and the definitions of $\frac{\partial x}{\partial r}, \frac{\partial z}{\partial r}, \frac{\partial \pi}{\partial r}, \frac{\partial S}{\partial r}$ are obvious. We also have

$$\frac{\partial \Lambda}{\partial L} = \sum_h \mu^h \frac{\partial V^h}{\partial l^h} - v\left(1 - \frac{\partial l^{p'}}{\partial x}\frac{\partial x}{\partial l} - \frac{\partial l^z}{\partial z}\frac{\partial z}{\partial l}\right) + \sigma\frac{\partial \pi}{\partial L} + \rho\frac{\partial S}{\partial L} = 0. \tag{3}$$

(2) and (3) may be rewritten as

$$\begin{pmatrix} -\left(\frac{\partial l^{p'}}{\partial x}\frac{\partial x}{\partial r} + \frac{\partial l^z}{\partial z}\frac{\partial z}{\partial r}\right) & 1 - \frac{\partial \pi}{\partial r} \\ \left(1 - \frac{\partial l^{p'}}{\partial x}\frac{\partial x}{\partial l} - \frac{\partial l^z}{\partial z}\frac{\partial z}{\partial l}\right) & -\frac{\partial \pi}{\partial L} \end{pmatrix} \cdot \begin{pmatrix} v \\ \sigma \end{pmatrix} = \begin{pmatrix} \sum_h \mu^h\theta^h \frac{\partial V^h}{\partial r^h} + \rho\frac{\partial S}{\partial r} \\ \sum_h \mu^h\theta^h \frac{\partial V^h}{\partial l^h} + \rho\frac{\partial S}{\partial L} \end{pmatrix} \tag{4}$$

and thus $(v \quad \sigma)$ is solution of

$$\begin{pmatrix} v \\ \sigma \end{pmatrix} = M \begin{pmatrix} \sum_h \mu^h\theta^h \frac{\partial V^h}{\partial r^h} + \rho\frac{\partial S}{\partial r} \\ \sum_h \mu^h\theta^h \frac{\partial V^h}{\partial l^h} + \rho\frac{\partial S}{\partial L} \end{pmatrix} \tag{5}$$

where M is a matrix of multipliers and is equal to the inverse of the matrix appearing on the left-hand side of (4).

Taking now the first derivatives of the Lagrangean with respect to q yields

$$\frac{\partial \Lambda}{\partial q} = \sum_h \mu^h \frac{\partial V^h}{\partial q} + v\left(\frac{\partial x}{\partial q}\frac{\partial l^p}{\partial x} + \frac{\partial l^z}{\partial z}\frac{\partial z}{\partial q}\right) + \rho\frac{\partial S}{\partial q} + \sigma\frac{\partial \pi}{\partial q} = 0 \tag{6}$$

$$= \sum_h \mu^h \frac{\partial V^h}{\partial q} + v\frac{\partial L}{\partial q} + \rho\frac{\partial S}{\partial q} + \sigma\frac{\partial \pi}{\partial q}. \tag{7}$$

Combining (5) and (7), and defining M_{ij} $(i, j = 1, 2)$ as the elements of M, one obtains

$$\begin{aligned} &\rho\left[\frac{\partial S}{\partial q} + \frac{\partial S}{\partial r}\left(\frac{\partial L}{\partial q}M_{11} + \frac{\partial \pi}{\partial q}M_{21}\right) + \frac{\partial S}{\partial L}\left(\frac{\partial L}{\partial q}M_{12} + \frac{\partial \pi}{\partial q}M_{22}\right)\right] \\ &\quad = -\sum_h \mu^h\left[\frac{\partial V^h}{\partial q} + \theta^h\frac{\partial V^h}{\partial r^h}\left(\frac{\partial L}{\partial q}M_{11} + \frac{\partial \pi}{\partial q}M_{21}\right)\right. \\ &\qquad \left. + \frac{\partial V^h}{\partial l^h}\left(\frac{\partial L}{\partial q}M_{12} + \frac{\partial \pi}{\partial q}M_{22}\right)\right]. \end{aligned} \tag{8}$$

If we define

$$\frac{d\pi}{dq} = \frac{\partial L}{\partial q} M_{11} + \frac{\partial \pi}{\partial q} M_{21}$$

$$\frac{dL}{dq} = \frac{\partial L}{\partial q} M_{12} + \frac{\partial \pi}{\partial q} M_{22},$$

we may combine (2.33) and (8) to obtain

$$\rho\left(\frac{\partial S}{\partial q} + \frac{\partial S}{\partial r}\frac{d\pi}{dq} + \frac{\partial S}{\partial L}\frac{dL}{dq}\right) = \sum_h \mu^h \varphi^h \left(C^h - \theta^h \frac{d\pi}{dq} - \frac{\psi^h}{\varphi^h}\frac{dl^h}{dq}\right). \tag{9}$$

Let us now define the reservation wage of agent h as

$$q_R^h = -\frac{\partial u^h}{\partial l} \bigg/ \frac{\partial V^h}{\partial r^h}.$$

We know that $\frac{\partial u^h}{\partial l} = \psi^h - \varphi^h(q_l - a)$ and $\frac{\partial V^h}{\partial r^h} = \varphi^h$, so that

$$q_R^h = \frac{\varphi^h(q_l - a) - \psi^h}{\varphi^h}$$

and

$$\frac{\psi^h}{\varphi^h} = (q_l - a - q_R^h).$$

The right-hand side of (9) may now be written as

$$\sum_h \mu^h \varphi^h \left[C^h - \theta^h \frac{d\pi}{dq} - (q_l - a - q_R^h)\frac{dl^h}{dq}\right]. \qquad \text{Q.E.D.}$$

3 Non-convexity of the mixed case with respect to 'pure' cases

We may take a convex combination of the vectors characterising the 'total' variation of an agent's utility in the Keynesian and the classical regime respectively (see (2.38) and (2.54))

$$\lambda\left(C^h - \theta^h \frac{d\pi}{dq} - \omega^h \frac{dL}{dq}\right) + (1-\lambda)\left(C^h - \omega^h \frac{dl^z}{dq}\right) \tag{1}$$

where $0 \leqslant \lambda \leqslant 1$

$$\frac{dl^z}{dq} = \left(1 - \frac{\partial l^z}{\partial z}\frac{\partial z}{\partial l}\right)^{-1}\left(\frac{\partial l^z}{\partial z}\frac{\partial z}{\partial q}\right)$$

$$\omega^h = (q_l - a - q_R^h).$$

(1) may be rewritten as

$$C^h - \lambda\theta^h \frac{d\pi}{dq} - \omega^h \frac{dl^z}{dq} + \lambda\omega^h\left(\frac{dl^z}{dq} - \frac{dL}{dq}\right). \tag{2}$$

We want to check whether there exists a λ $(0 \leqslant \lambda \leqslant 1)$ such that (2) equals (2.66), i.e.

$$\lambda\left[\theta^h \frac{d\pi}{dq} - \omega^h\left(\frac{dl^z}{dq} - \frac{dL}{dq}\right)\right] + \omega^h \frac{dl^z}{dq} = \theta_1^h \frac{d\pi_x}{dq} + \omega^h \frac{dL^K}{dq} \tag{3}$$

or,
$$\forall i: \lambda = \left[\theta^h \frac{d\pi}{dq_i} + \omega^h\left(\frac{dL}{dq_i} - \frac{dl^z}{dq_i}\right)\right]^{-1}\left[\theta_1^h \frac{d\pi_x}{dq_i} + \omega^h\left(\frac{dL^K}{dq_i} - \frac{dl^z}{dq_i}\right)\right] \tag{4}$$

Generally this latter expression cannot be satisfied simultaneously for all i's. Q.E.D.

4 Hours worked

(i) *Effective duration of work* (EDW): this series concerns blue-collars and is computed by dividing the total number of hours worked by the number of blue-collars on the payroll;

(ii) *Conventional duration of work* (CDW): this series is based on the 'collective conventions'

	EDW per year	CDW per year
1953	2140	2336
54	2147	2335
55	2150	2332
56	2114	2298
57	2042	2274
58	2025	2274
59	2018	2262
60	2045	2236
61	2018	2227
62	2049	2225
63	2066	2223
64	2043	2209

	EDW per year	CDW per year
65	1995	2157
66	1973	2129
67	1942	2102
68	1950	2093
69	1933	2061
70	1877	2024
71	1849	2008
72	1788	1975
73	1758	1926
74	1702	1887
75	1584	1859
76	1600	1847
77	1579	1840
78	1575	1836
79	1564	1827
80	1549	1792
81	1503	1790
82	1505	1784

Source: Bureau du Plan, MARIBEL.

5 Production sectors

Items	NACE code
1. Agriculture	011–013–014–019–020–030
2. Coal	111–112
3. Coking	120
4. Oil	130–140
5. Electricity	161–163
6. Gas (distribution)	162
7. Water	170
8. Mining (iron)	211–221–222–223
9. Mining (non-iron)	151–152–212–224
10. Glass	247
11. Cement	242–243
12. Non-metallic ore	231–232–233–241–244–245–246–248
13. Chemicals	252–253–255–256–257–258–259–260
14. Metallic products	311 to 316
15. Agricultural machinery	321 to 328
16. Office equipment	330–371 to 374
17. Electrical material	341 to 346
18. Automobile	351 to 353

Items	NACE code
19. Transports (other than auto.)	361 to 365
20. Meat	412
21. Milk	413
22. Food	411–414 to 423
23. Beverage	424 to 428
24. Tobacco	429
25. Textile (clothing)	436–453
26. Other textile	431–432–438–439–455–456
27. Leather	441–442–451
28. Wood	461 to 467
29. Paper	471 to 474
30. Rubber	481–482
31. Plastics	483
32. Manufacturing industries	491 to 495
33. Construction	505–506–507–509
34. Repair of vehicles	671
35. Recuperation	620–672
36. Commercial services	610–630–640
37. Hotels and restaurants	660
38. Trains, trams and buses	710–721
39. Road transports	722 to 725
40. Inland navigation	730
41. High-sea navigation	741–742
42. Air freight	750
43. Other transportation services	761 to 764, 771 to 773
44. Communication services	790
45. Credit and insurance	811 to 813, 820
46. Other services	830–840–92C–93C–94C–96B–97B 981 to 984
47. Rents	850
48. Health	95(A, B, C)
49. Public administration	91–92A–96A–97A
50. Education	93A–93B–94A–94B

6 Distribution matrix

Production sectors	Food	Clothing	Housing	Energy	Communic.	Durables	Services	Exog. dem.	Exports
1	0.14960	0.00000	0.00000	0.00260	0.00000	0.00000	0.02700	−0.00196	0.01829
2	0.00000	0.00000	0.00000	0.08450	0.00000	0.00000	0.00000	0.00148	0.00077
3	0.00000	0.00000	0.00000	0.00120	0.00000	0.00000	0.00000	−0.00039	0.00095
4	0.00000	0.00000	0.00000	0.59340	0.00000	0.00000	0.00046	−0.00094	0.04261
5	0.00000	0.00000	0.00000	0.22400	0.00000	0.00000	0.00030	0.00000	0.00171
6	0.00000	0.00000	0.00000	0.09000	0.00000	0.00000	0.00000	−0.00005	0.00001
7	0.00000	0.00000	0.02100	0.00000	0.00000	0.00000	0.00000	0.00000	0.00000
8	0.00000	0.00000	0.00000	0.00000	0.00000	0.00180	0.00000	−0.00642	0.08816
9	0.00000	0.00000	0.00000	0.00000	0.00000	0.00070	0.00000	0.00295	0.03995
10	0.00000	0.00000	0.00047	0.00000	0.00000	0.02800	0.00000	−0.00001	0.00945
11	0.00000	0.00000	0.00000	0.00000	0.00000	0.00000	0.00013	−0.00231	0.00428
12	0.00040	0.00000	0.00510	0.00000	0.00000	0.00000	0.00170	−0.00261	0.00510
13	0.00000	0.00000	0.05300	0.00000	0.00000	0.00000	0.13200	−0.00082	0.10711
14	0.00000	0.00000	0.00140	0.00000	0.00000	0.07700	0.00090	−0.00919	0.02248
15	0.00000	0.00000	0.00000	0.00000	0.00000	0.01300	0.00000	0.01836	0.06615
16	0.00000	0.03700	0.00000	0.00000	0.00000	0.00890	0.00560	0.00106	0.00397
17	0.00000	0.00000	0.00470	0.00000	0.00000	0.11600	0.00000	0.03753	0.04132
18	0.00000	0.00000	0.00000	0.00000	0.00000	0.17862	0.00000	0.00799	0.08595
19	0.00000	0.00000	0.00000	0.00000	0.00000	0.01190	0.00030	0.01294	0.00907
20	0.29540	0.00000	0.00000	0.00000	0.00000	0.00000	0.00000	−0.00017	0.02063
21	0.09400	0.00000	0.00000	0.00000	0.00000	0.00000	0.00000	0.00389	0.00794
22	0.23000	0.00000	0.00100	0.00000	0.00000	0.00000	0.00000	0.00082	0.02785
23	0.06670	0.00000	0.00000	0.00000	0.00000	0.00000	0.00000	−0.00016	0.00544

24	0.06620	0.00000	0.00000	0.00000	0.00000	0.00000	0.00000	0.00020	0.00405
25	0.00000	0.73480	0.00780	0.00000	0.00000	0.00000	0.00040	−0.00044	0.02177
26	0.00000	0.01000	0.00020	0.00000	0.00000	0.12530	0.00200	−0.00080	0.05444
27	0.00000	0.17260	0.00022	0.00000	0.00000	0.00000	0.00000	0.00006	0.00415
28	0.00000	0.00000	0.00310	0.00600	0.00000	0.20900	0.00070	0.00141	0.01637
29	0.00000	0.00000	0.00990	0.00000	0.00000	0.00000	0.04700	−0.00583	0.02256
30	0.00000	0.00000	0.00000	0.00000	0.00000	0.12130	0.00330	0.00012	0.00475
31	0.00000	0.00000	0.00023	0.00000	0.00000	0.00000	0.02400	−0.00040	0.01111
32	0.00000	0.04500	0.00006	0.00000	0.00000	0.00375	0.03260	0.00045	0.01023
33	0.00000	0.00000	0.02400	0.00000	0.00000	0.00000	0.00000	0.35117	0.00579
34	0.00000	0.00000	0.00000	0.00000	0.00000	0.13170	0.00000	0.00000	0.00000
35	0.00000	0.00000	0.05220	0.00000	0.00000	0.00040	0.00300	−0.00754	0.00396
36	0.00000	0.00000	0.00000	0.00000	0.00000	0.00000	0.00000	0.01163	0.05666
37	0.09770	0.00000	0.00000	0.00000	0.00000	0.00000	0.21400	0.00000	0.00193
38	0.00000	0.00000	0.00000	0.00000	0.41300	0.00000	0.00000	0.00008	0.00373
39	0.00000	0.00000	0.00620	0.00000	0.13800	0.00000	0.00000	0.00077	0.01106
40	0.00000	0.00000	0.00000	0.00000	0.00000	0.00000	0.00000	0.00006	0.00371
41	0.00000	0.00000	0.00000	0.00000	0.01550	0.00000	0.00000	0.00000	0.01418
42	0.00000	0.00000	0.00000	0.00000	0.03580	0.00000	0.00000	0.00000	0.00808
43	0.00000	0.00000	0.00013	0.00000	0.00000	0.00000	0.00360	0.00034	0.03632
44	0.00000	0.00000	0.00000	0.00000	0.39800	0.00000	0.00000	0.00000	0.00174
45	0.00000	0.00000	0.00520	0.00000	0.00000	0.03120	0.06110	0.00000	0.00133
46	0.00000	0.00000	0.25660	0.00000	0.00000	0.00000	0.14060	0.01812	0.02896
47	0.00000	0.00000	0.54700	0.00000	0.00000	0.01440	0.00000	0.00000	0.00000
48	0.00000	0.00000	0.00000	0.00000	0.00000	0.00000	0.29880	0.00000	0.00000
49	0.00000	0.00000	0.00000	0.00000	0.00000	0.00000	0.00000	0.25083	0.00000
50	0.00000	0.00000	0.00000	0.00000	0.00000	0.00000	0.00000	0.17779	0.00000
51	0.00000	0.00000	0.00000	0.00000	0.00000	0.00000	0.00000	0.12167	0.06895

7 Transition matrix

Production sectors	Food	Clothing	Housing	Energy	Communic.	Durables	Services	Exog. dem.	Exports
1	0.18979	0.00091	0.00123	0.00192	0.00021	0.00297	0.01846	0.00087	0.01847
2	0.00040	0.00024	0.00039	0.06050	0.00125	0.00086	0.00047	0.00169	0.00476
3	0.00002	0.00002	0.00006	0.00014	0.00015	0.00019	0.00002	0.00011	0.00141
4	0.00487	0.00204	0.00313	0.18115	0.00742	0.00379	0.00529	0.00311	0.01644
5	0.00908	0.00575	0.00471	0.14391	0.01805	0.01065	0.01098	0.00654	0.01308
6	0.00127	0.00059	0.00083	0.08600	0.00151	0.00149	0.00182	0.00124	0.00388
7	0.00288	0.00031	0.01951	0.00039	0.00078	0.00059	0.00646	0.00145	0.00093
8	0.00034	0.00025	0.00121	0.00040	0.00337	0.00396	0.00035	0.00281	0.02982
9	0.00010	0.00013	0.00019	0.00003	0.00009	0.00089	0.00032	0.00106	0.00760
10	0.00097	0.00029	0.00079	0.00009	0.00021	0.01783	0.00075	0.00173	0.00629
11	0.00047	0.00021	0.00367	0.00132	0.00114	0.00048	0.00090	0.01185	0.00313
12	0.00147	0.00018	0.00527	0.00031	0.00133	0.00080	0.00177	0.00669	0.00403
13	0.00514	0.00170	0.01915	0.00082	0.00121	0.00498	0.04887	0.00095	0.03886
14	0.00561	0.00316	0.00394	0.00271	0.00486	0.05013	0.00396	0.01557	0.02055
15	0.00172	0.00086	0.00103	0.00180	0.00162	0.00932	0.00091	0.01259	0.03365
16	0.00002	0.02281	0.00002	0.00002	0.00009	0.00552	0.00355	0.00071	0.00248
17	0.00019	0.00060	0.00305	0.00013	0.00564	0.06205	0.00047	0.02186	0.02556
18	0.00002	0.00001	0.00001	0.00001	0.00019	0.04074	0.00001	0.00185	0.01957
19	0.00013	0.00002	0.00003	0.00064	0.00042	0.00657	0.00020	0.00773	0.00511
20	0.05710	0.00034	0.00020	0.00002	0.00002	0.00006	0.00175	0.00005	0.00408
21	0.01407	0.00001	0.00003	0.00001	0.00000	0.00001	0.00039	0.00056	0.00121
22	0.10232	0.00021	0.00066	0.00035	0.00005	0.00059	0.00579	0.00048	0.01166
23	0.04509	0.00019	0.00010	0.00007	0.00007	0.00018	0.01851	0.00004	0.00340

24	0.04736	0.00000	0.00003	0.00000	0.00000	0.00001	0.00007	0.00024	0.00290
25	0.00015	0.35679	0.00393	0.00009	0.00210	0.00038	0.00047	0.00017	0.01085
26	0.00040	0.03211	0.00057	0.00006	0.00038	0.05080	0.00141	0.00010	0.02233
27	0.00000	0.07411	0.00014	0.00001	0.00000	0.00007	0.00002	0.00003	0.00181
28	0.00051	0.00033	0.00352	0.00300	0.00308	0.09876	0.00129	0.00590	0.00861
29	0.01039	0.00546	0.01201	0.00180	0.00369	0.00746	0.03235	0.00294	0.01746
30	0.00014	0.00012	0.00019	0.00003	0.00057	0.05838	0.00176	0.00043	0.00270
31	0.00117	0.00147	0.00089	0.00009	0.00035	0.00240	0.01113	0.00122	0.00561
32	0.00005	0.01800	0.00020	0.00003	0.00005	0.00209	0.01309	0.00061	0.00457
33	0.00257	0.00198	0.04919	0.00265	0.00266	0.00386	0.00620	0.18307	0.00548
34	0.00390	0.00161	0.00157	0.00076	0.00621	0.07307	0.00244	0.00177	0.00275
35	0.00033	0.00024	0.04476	0.00017	0.00050	0.00352	0.00300	−0.00579	0.00625
36	0.03003	0.01129	0.01059	0.00265	0.01643	0.02368	0.03097	0.03007	0.06116
37	0.05476	0.00097	0.00026	0.00038	0.00034	0.00092	0.11936	0.00061	0.00176
38	0.00067	0.00124	0.00052	0.00079	0.24176	0.00097	0.00084	0.00281	0.00327
39	0.00997	0.00803	0.00780	0.00259	0.10784	0.01188	0.00542	0.00775	0.01508
40	0.00112	0.00006	0.00027	0.00027	0.00054	0.00038	0.00039	0.00055	0.00351
41	0.00001	0.00000	0.00000	0.00000	0.00736	0.00001	0.00001	0.00001	0.00670
42	0.00016	0.00042	0.00009	0.00015	0.01357	0.00045	0.00017	0.00010	0.00336
43	0.01075	0.00213	0.00222	0.00218	0.00372	0.00731	0.00853	0.00358	0.04439
44	0.00402	0.00412	0.00599	0.00242	0.35212	0.00756	0.01329	0.00569	0.00682
45	0.00157	0.00150	0.00585	0.00035	0.00253	0.01028	0.01781	0.00260	0.00198
46	0.03109	0.01639	0.21610	0.01372	0.01611	0.03568	0.14893	0.04341	0.04223
47	0.00000	0.00000	0.46615	0.00000	0.00000	0.00972	0.00000	0.00232	0.00000
48	0.00437	0.00003	0.00014	0.00023	0.00054	0.00011	0.21894	0.00088	0.00047
49	0.00000	0.00000	0.00000	0.00000	0.00000	0.00000	0.00000	0.17644	0.00000
50	0.00000	0.00000	0.00000	0.00000	0.00000	0.00000	0.00000	0.15329	0.00000
51	0.34142	0.42018	0.09735	0.48456	0.16814	0.43592	0.22960	0.27767	0.45000

8 Tax rates

V.A.T. rates in 1982 (in %)

Food	6.16
Beverage	20.20
Tobacco	6.00
Clothing	18.14
Rents and water	1.41
Heating, lighting	16.22
Durables	18.97
Non-durables	10.04
Communications	11.74
Leisure	12.46
Financial services	4.31
Education and research	6.44
Other services	1.16
Transportation equipment	24.86
Gasoline	25.00
Repair, tyres, . . .	17.00
Public transports	6.00
Average on private consumption	10.35

Source: Bureau du Plan.

Excise and other consumption taxes

	Tax paid ($\times 10^6$ BF)
Alcohol	9700
Coffee	564
Other beverages	6171
Tobacco	23172
Gasoline	39190
Sugar	251

Source: I.N.S. (1984).

9 Generating vectors of $\Lambda^* \cap S^{\perp}$

	1	2	3	4	5	6
Food	−0.466	−0.737	−0.567	−0.224	−0.073	0.096
Durables	−0.156	−0.234	−0.948	−0.925	−0.490	0.146
Energy	−1.155	0.150	1.791	−0.604	−2.036	−1.528
Housing	−0.214	−0.537	−0.888	−0.848	−0.414	0.412
Services	−0.211	0.077	0.204	0.560	0.299	−0.583
Communications	0.000	2.358	4.188	3.293	0.756	−2.914
Clothing	7.395	5.570	1.376	3.483	5.697	4.133
Labour	0.403	0.338	−0.039	0.063	0.235	0.188

	7	8	9	10	11	12
Food	−0.394	−1.228	−0.425	−1.270	0.183	0.028
Durables	−0.366	−2.210	−0.378	−2.446	0.537	0.264
Energy	0.770	1.824	0.284	1.072	−1.759	−1.185
Housing	−0.046	1.277	0.428	1.906	0.546	0.538
Services	0.000	1.049	0.000	0.970	−1.062	−0.793
Communications	6.743	0.000	6.470	0.000	−1.686	−3.190
Clothing	−1.574	−2.015	−1.887	−1.894	4.015	3.829
Labour	−0.108	−0.396	−0.128	−0.442	0.212	0.173

	13	14	15	16	17	18
Food	−0.627	−0.412	−0.542	−0.771	−0.914	−0.880
Durables	−0.960	−0.716	−0.864	−1.465	−0.399	−0.335
Energy	2.312	0.000	0.592	−0.191	2.924	2.792
Housing	−0.866	−0.114	−0.218	1.649	−0.720	−0.720
Services	0.077	−1.302	−1.062	0.125	0.068	0.000
Communications	4.375	0.000	0.000	−3.819	4.816	5.186
Clothing	0.691	7.295	6.601	1.817	−0.146	−0.085
Labout	−0.092	0.160	0.121	−0.163	−0.012	−0.002

	19	20	21	22	23	24
Food	−1.158	−0.629	−0.634	−0.547	−0.662	0.060
Durables	0.168	−1.153	−1.110	−1.029	−1.186	0.271
Energy	2.795	1.536	1.783	1.461	1.643	−1.218
Housing	−0.313	0.459	0.207	0.275	0.449	0.573
Services	−0.425	0.814	0.774	0.688	0.849	−0.820
Communications	3.411	1.754	2.178	2.592	1.572	−3.298
Clothing	1.576	−3.343	−3.030	−3.122	−3.327	3.608
Labour	0.154	−0.312	−0.285	−0.286	−0.313	0.151

	25	26	27	28	29	30
Food	−0.493	−0.650	−0.595	−0.644	−0.510	−0.525
Durables	−0.848	−1.131	−1.065	−1.161	0.099	0.225
Energy	2.439	2.805	1.730	1.636	2.398	2.365
Housing	−0.527	−0.524	0.284	0.455	0.095	0.218
Services	−0.330	−0.799	0.714	0.819	−0.599	−0.731
Communications	3.725	3.753	1.949	1.543	2.401	2.033
Clothing	−1.341	0.000	−3.351	−3.421	−3.596	−3.603
Labour	−0.296	−0.338	−0.312	−0.321	−0.302	−0.300

	31	32	33
Food	−0.283	−0.135	−0.701
Durables	−0.720	−0.458	−0.592
Energy	−0.955	−1.511	1.746
Housing	−0.349	0.605	−0.821
Services	−0.343	−0.162	0.306
Communications	0.000	−2.758	4.338
Clothing	7.103	4.242	1.439
Labour	0.248	0.130	0.056

References

ABBOTT, M. and O. ASHENFELTER (1976), 'Labour supply, commodity demand and the allocation of time', *Review of Economic Studies*, **43**, 389–411.

AHMAD, E. and N. STERN (1984), 'The theory of tax reform and Indian indirect taxes', *Journal of Public Economics*, **25**, 259–98.

ARROW, K. and F. HAHN (1971), *General Competitive Analysis*, Amsterdam, North-Holland.

ASHENFELTER, O. (1980), 'Unemployment as disequilibrium in a model of aggregate labour supply', *Econometrica*, **48,** 547–64.

AZARIADIS, C. and J. STIGLITZ (1983), 'Implicit contracts and fixed-price equilibria', *Quarterly Journal of Economics* (supplement).

BAILY, M.N. (1974), 'Wages and employment under uncertain demand', *Review of Economic Studies*, **40**, 37–40.

Banque Nationale de Belgique (1980), 'L'essouflement de l'économie belge dans la décennie passée', Bruxelles.

(1982), *Bulletin de la B.N.B.*, LVII Année, Tome II, no 1–2, juillet–août, Bruxelles.

BARRO, B.J. and H.I. GROSSMAN (1971), 'A general disequilibrium model of income and employment', *American Economic Review*, **41**, 82–93.

BARTEN, A. (1969), 'Maximum likelihood estimation of a complete system of demand equations', *European Economic Review*, **1** (1), 7–73.

BAUMOL, W.J. and D.F. BRADFORD (1970), 'Optimal departures from marginal cost pricing', *American Economic Review*, **40**, 265–83.

BAZARAA, M.S. and C.W. SHETTY (1976), *Foundations of Optimization*, Berlin, Springer-Verlag.

BENASSY, J.P. (1973), 'Disequilibrium T heory'. Ph.D. dissertation, University of California, Berkeley.

(1975), 'Neo-Keynesian disequilibrium theory in a monetary economy', *Review of Economic Studies*, **42**, 503–23.

(1976), 'The disequilibrium approach to monopolistic price setting and general monopolistic equilibrium', *Review of Economic Studies*, **43**, 69–81.

BOITEUX, M. (1956), 'Sur la gestion des monopoles publics astreints à l'équilibre budgétaire', *Econometrica*, **24** (1), 22–40.

BRONSARD, C. and L. SALVAS-BRONSARD (1980) 'Sur les différentes formes structurelles engendrées par la théorie de la demande et leur utilisation en économétrie: Systèmes direct, réciproque, mixte et système avec rationnement quantitatif', *Annales de l'INSEE*, **40**, 3–32.

BRONSARD, C. and E. WAGNEUR (1980), 'Second rang et déséquilibre', *Cahier 8041 du Centre de Sciences Economiques et Centre de Recherche en Développement Economique*, Université de Montréal.

Bureau du Plan (1982), *Matrices Input-Output 1965, 1970 et 1975*, Bruzelles.

(1984), 'Maribel', *Note technique*, Bruzelles.

(1985), 'Dossier Maribel', *Note technique* ME/3494/A1/4448, Bruxelles.

CARLTON, D.W. (1986), 'The rigidity of prices', *American Economic Review*, **76**, 637–58.

CLOWER, R.W. (1965), 'The Keynesian counterrevolution: a theoretical appraisal', in F.H. Hahn and F.P. Brechling, eds., *The Theory of Interest Rates*, London, Macmillan.

D'ALCANTARA, G. (1983), 'SERENA: *A Macroeconomic Sectoral Regional and National Accounting Econometric Model for the Belgian Economy*', Katholieke Universiteit te Leuven.

DASGUPTA, P., S.A. MARGLIN and A.K. SEN (1972), *Guidelines for Project Evaluation*, United Nations, UNIDO.

DASGUPTA, P. and J. STIGLITZ (1972), 'On optimal taxation and public taxation', *Review of Economic Studies*, **39**, 87–103.

D'ASPREMONT, C. and H. TULKENS (1980), 'Commodity exchanges as gradient processes', *Econometrica*, **48** (2), 387–99.

DAVIDSON, J., D. HENDRY, F. SRBA and S. YEO (1978), 'Econometric modelling of the aggregate time-series relationship between consumers' expenditure and income in the U.K.', *The Economic Journal*, **88**, 661–92.

DEATON, A. (1981), 'Theoretical and empirical approaches to consumer demand under rationing', in: *Essays in the Theory and Measurement of Consumer Behaviour*, Cambridge, Cambridge University Press.

DIAMOND, P. and J. MIRRLEES (1971), 'Optimal taxation and public production: I. Production efficiency, II. Tax rules', *American Economic Review*, **61**, 8–27 and 261–78.

DIEWERT, W.E. (1983), 'Cost benefit analysis and project evaluation: a comparison of alternative approaches', *Journal of Public Economics*, **22**, 265–302.

DIXIT, A.K. (1970), 'On the optimum structure of commodity taxes', *American Economic Review*, **40**, 295–301.

(1975), 'Welfare effects of tax and price changes', *Journal of Public Economics*, **4**, 103–23.

(1976), 'Public finance in a Keynesian temporary disequilibrium', *Journal of Economic Theory*, **12**, 242–58.

DIXIT, A.K. and K. MUNK (1977), 'Welfare effects of tax and price changes: a correction', *Journal of Public Economics*, **8**, 103–7.

DRÈZE, J.H. (1964), 'Some post-war contributions of French economists to theory and public policy'. *merican Economics*, **8**, 103–7.

(1975), 'Existence of an equilibrium under price rigidity and quantity rationing', *International Economic Review*, **16**, 301–20.

(1984), 'Second-best analysis with markets in disequilibrium: public sector pricing in a Keynesian regime', in: *The Performance of Public Enterprises*, M. Marchand *et al.* (eds.), Amsterdam, Elsevier–North-Holland.

DRÈZE, J.H. and F. MODIGLIANI (1981). 'The trade-off between real wages and employment in an open Economy (Belgium)', *European Economic Review*, **15**, 1–40.

DRÈZE, J.H. and H. SNEESSENS (1986), 'A discussion of Belgian unemployment, combining traditional concepts and disequilibrium economics', *Economica*, **53** (supplement).

FELDSTEIN, M. (1975), 'On the theory of tax reform', *Journal of Public Economics*, **6**, 77–104.

FELDSTEIN, M. and J. POTERBA (1984), 'Unemployment insurance and reservation wages', *Journal of Public Economics*, **23**, 141–68.

GINSBURGH, V. and L. VANDER HEYDEN (1985), 'General equilibrium and wage rigidities: an application to Belgium', *Mathematical Programming Study*, **23**, 23–39.

GUESNERIE, R. (1977), 'On the direction of tax reform', *Journal of Public Economics*, **7**, 179–202.

GUESNERIE, R. and J. TIROLE (1981), 'Tax reform from the gradient projection viewpoint', *Journal of Public Economics*, **15**, 275–93.

HAMMOND, P.J. (1986), 'Project evaluation by potential tax reform', *Journal of Public Economics*, **30**, 1–36.

HARRIS, R. and J. MACKINNON (1979), 'Computing optimal tax equilibria', *Journal of Public Economics*, **11**, 197–212.

HART, O. (1982), 'A model of imperfect competition with Keynesian features', *The Quarterly Journal of Economics*, **97**, 109–38.

HENDRY, D. and J.-F. RICHARD (1983), 'The econometric analysis of economic time series', *International Statistical Review*, **51**, 111–63.

I.N.S. (1982), *Annuaire Statistique*, Ministère des Affaires Economiques, Royaume de Belgique.

(1983), *Tableau entrées-sorties de la Belgique pour 1975*, Ministère des Affaires Economiques, Royaume de Belgique.

(1984), *Enquête sur le budget des ménages 1978–1979*, Tome V, Ministère des Affaires Economiques, Royaume de Belgique.

JOHANSSON, P.O. (1982), 'Cost benefit rules in general disequilibrium', *Journal of Public Economics*, **18**, 121–7.

LAMBERT, J.-P. (1986), *Disequilibrium Macro-models Based on Survey Data: Theory and Estimation for the Belgian Manufacturing Sector*, Cambridge, Cambridge University Press.

LEIJONHUFVUD, A. (1968), *On Keynesian Economics and the Economics of Keynes*, Oxford University Press.

LITTLE, I.M. and J.A. MIRRLEES (1974), *Project Appraisal and Planning for Developing Countries*, Basic Books, New York.

MALINVAUD, E. (1977), *The Theory of Unemployment Reconsidered*, Oxford, Basil Blackwell.

(1983), *Essais sur la théorie du chômage*, Paris, Calmann-Levy.

MALINVAUD, E. and Y. YOUNES (1978), 'Une nouvelle formulation générale pour l'étude des fondements microéconomiques de la macroéconomique', *Cahiers du Séminaire d'Économétrie*.

MEULDERS, D. and R. TOLLET (1975), 'Inégalité et la structure des revenus en Belgique', *Cahiers Economiques de Bruxelles*, **67**, 317–52.

Ministère des Finances (1984), *Bulletin du Ministère des Finances*, Royaume de Belgique.

MOOKHERJEE, D. (1986), 'Shadow pricing with suboptimal policy rules', *Journal of Public Economics*, **31**, 287–305.

MUELLBAUER, J. and R. PORTES (1978), 'Macroeconomic models with quantity rationing', *Economic Journal*, **88**, 788–821.

MUNK, K. (1978), 'Optimal taxation and pure profits', *Scandinavian Journal of Economics*, **80**, 1–19.

NEGISHI, T. (1971), *General Equilibrium and International Trade*, Amsterdam, North-Holland.

OECD (1984), *Belgique–Luxembourg*, Études économiques de l'OECD, Paris, OECD.

PHLIPS, L. (1974), *Applied Consumption Analysis*, Amsterdam–New-York, North-Holland/Elsevier.

(1978), 'The demand for leisure and money', *Econometrica*, **46** (5), 1025–43.

PICARD, P. (1981), 'Prix fictifs et déséquilibre en économie ouverte', *Cahiers du Séminaire d'Econométrie*, **25**, 139–85.

PIERAERTS, P. and L. PHLIPS (1978), 'Loisirs et salaires réels en Belgique', Working paper 7811, Institut des Sciences Economiques, Université Catholique de Louvain.

PIGOU, A.C. (1947), *A Study in Public Finance*, 3rd Edition, London, MacMillan.

PRESTON, R.S. (1972), *The Wharton Annual and Industry Forecasting Model*, Wharton School, University of Pennsylvania.

RAMSEY, F.P. (1927), 'A contribution to the theory of taxation', *Economic Journal*, **37**, 47–61.

ROBERT, F., F.X. DE DONNÉA, M. MARCHAND and H. TULKENS (1983), 'Entreprises et services publics: Évolution institutionnelle générale et dix-neuf études de cas (1950–1980)', *Bulletin de Documentation du Ministère des Finances*, Bruxelles.

SAMUELSON, P.A. (1951), 'Theory of optimal taxation', appeared in the *Journal of Public Economics*, 1986, **30**, 137–44.

SANDMO, A. (1976), 'Optimal taxation', *Journal of Public Economics*, **6**, 37–54.

SEN, A. (1970), *Collective Choice and Social Welfare*, San Francisco, Holden-Day.

SIMON, W.W. (1965), 'Personnel consumption expenditure in 1958: input–output study', *Survey of Economic Business*, **45** (10), 7–20.

SNEESSENS, H. (1981), *Theory and Estimation of Macroeconomic Rationing Models*, Berlin, Springer-Verlag.

STEPHENSON, S.P. (1976), 'The economics of youth search behaviour', *The Review of Economics and Statistics*, **58**, 104–11.

VAN ROMPUY, P. (1969), *De Vraag naar arbeid*, Antwerpen-Utrecht, Standaard Wetenschappelijke Uitgeverij.

WEYMARK, J. (1979), 'A reconciliation of recent results in optimal taxation theory', *Journal of Public Economics*, **12**, 171–89.

(1980), 'Undominated directions of tax reforms', *Journal of Public Economics*, **16**, 343–69.

YOUNES, Y. (1975), 'On the role of money in the process of exchange and the existence of non-Walrasian equilibrium', *Review of Economic Studies*, **42**, 489–501.

Index